THE PARISH PSALTER
WITH CHANTS

THE PSALMS OF DAVID POINTED
FOR CHANTING

BY

SYDNEY H. NICHOLSON

THE ROYAL SCHOOL OF CHURCH MUSIC

First published January 1932
Re-set 1989
Printed 1991
Reprinted 1992
Reprinted 1993
Reprinted 1995
Reprinted 1998
Reprinted 1999
Reprinted 2006

RSCM ISBN 0 854020 91 8
(formerly Addington Press
ISBN 0 906851 00 9)

Musical art-work by
G. E. King
MSS Studios
Rhiwlas, Cae Deintur
Dolgellau, Gwynedd
LL40 2YS

Printed by
Halstan & Co. Ltd., Amersham, Bucks., England

REVISED PREFACE, 1989

THE original preface to The Parish Psalter, which was first published sixty years ago, gave detailed explanations of the principles governing the then new way of approaching the singing of psalms.

Today, although the principles underlying 'speech rhythm' are widely understood, they are not always put into practice correctly; for the freedom of the method allows such a wide measure of flexibility that it is open to many and varied interpretations.

It may therefore be helpful to set out some general guide-lines which need constantly to be borne in mind:

1 The basic purpose of The Parish Psalter is to secure the proper emphasis and rhythm of the words by the simplest means and with the minimum of signs. *Successful use of the Psalter consequently demands thought and sensitivity.*

2 Some of the most frequent inaccuracies occur when three or more syllables have to be sung to a bar of music containing only two notes. *The rule here is that the second note is reserved for the final syllable or word,* for example:

    Psalm 67, verse 1b   /merci   ful/

    Psalm 67, verse 3a   /praise thee O/

(In certain exceptional cases a dot indicates the division; see Psalm 1, verses 1b and 7a.)

3 In order to punctuate clearly and logically, breath should always be taken at commas.

4 In those instances where the reciting note is $\partial.$ $\downarrow$ (the second half of chant no. 67), instead of the more usual single note, *the crotchet must be sung to the last syllable or word before the bar line which follows.*

5 When an unimportant word or syllable (eg. the 'and' of Psalm 11, verse 3b) occurs on a reciting note, this should be sung lightly and quickly. *In all cases, the aim is to stress important words and syllables, while treating unimportant words and syllables lightly.*

6 An extra space between certain verses indicates a change of mood in the text and where a corresponding change of chant may be equally appropriate.

7 Verses marked by an asterisk (*) should preferably be sung through without a break at the colon (Psalm 122, verse 2). However, these verses are also printed at the foot of the page in normal pointing for those who prefer to use it.

8 The 'half-chant' sign (½) is employed in a few cases (Psalm 19, verse 15) to indicate that the chant should be commenced at the double bar. *This device is only practicable with single chants.*

9 Psalms 101, 115 and 148 are provided with special chants with fewer notes which aim to secure greater smoothness. (In the words-only edition, these psalms and chants are printed as an Appendix.) These psalms are also provided with ordinary chants and normal pointing.

10 In a few cases, descants are given but the use of these is entirely optional.

Finally, in order to obtain the best and most convincing results, it is helpful to read the words aloud first, phrasing them in a deliberate and thoughtful way.

July 1989

INDEX OF CHANTS

INDEX OF CHANTS—*continued*

VENITE, EXULTEMUS (Psalm 95) THE CANTICLES

f   O COME let us ' sing unto the ' Lord : let us heartily rejoice in the '
    strength of ' our sal'vation.

    2 Let us come before his ' presence with ' thanksgiving : and shew
    ourselves ' glad in ' him with ' psalms.

    3 For the Lord is a ' great ' God : and a great ' King above ' all ' gods.

    4 In his hand are all the ' corners · of the ' earth : and the strength of
    the ' hills is ' his ' also.

2nd   5 The sea is his and ' he ' made it : and his hands pre ' pared the '
Part   dry ' land.

p   6 O come let us worship and ' fall ' down : and kneel be'fore the '
    Lord our ' Maker.

    7 For he is the ' Lord our ' God : and we are the people of his pasture,
    and the ' sheep of ' his ' hand.

mf   8 To-day if ye will hear his voice, harden ' not your ' hearts : as in the
    provocation, and as in the day of temp'tation ' in the ' wilderness;

*   9 When your ' fathers ' tempted ' me : ' proved me and ' saw my '
    works.

    10 Forty years long was I grieved with this gene'ration and ' said : It
    is a people that do err in their hearts, for they ' have not '
    known my ' ways;

    11 Unto whom I ' sware · in my ' wrath : that they should not ' enter '
    into my ' rest.

    Glory be to the Father, and ' to the ' Son : and ' to the ' Holy ' Ghost;

    As it was in the beginning, is now and ' ever ' shall be : world without '
    end. ' A'men.

---

9 When your fathers ' tempted ' me : proved ' me and ' saw my ' works.

f   O COME let us ' sing unto the ' Lord : let us heartily rejoice in the '
strength of ' our sal'vation.

2 Let us come before his ' presence with ' thanksgiving : and shew
ourselves ' glad in ' him with ' psalms.

3 For the Lord is a ' great ' God : and a great ' King above ' all ' gods.

4 In his hand are all the ' corners · of the ' earth : and the strength of
the ' hills is ' his ' also.

2nd Part   5 The sea is his and ' he ' made it : and his hands pre ' pared the '
dry ' land.

p   6 O come let us worship and ' fall ' down : and kneel be'fore the '
Lord our ' Maker.

7 For he is the ' Lord our ' God : and we are the people of his pasture,
and the ' sheep of ' his ' hand.

mf   8 To-day if ye will hear his voice, harden ' not your ' hearts : as in the
provocation, and as in the day of temp'tation ' in the ' wilderness;

*   9 When your ' fathers ' tempted ' me : ' proved me and ' saw my '
works.

10 Forty years long was I grieved with this gene'ration and ' said : It
is a people that do err in their hearts, for they ' have not '
known my ' ways;

11 Unto whom I ' sware · in my ' wrath : that they should not ' enter '
into my ' rest.

Glory be to the Father, and ' to the ' Son : and ' to the ' Holy ' Ghost;

As it was in the beginning, is now and ' ever ' shall be : world without '
end. ' A'men.

---

9 When your fathers ' tempted ' me : proved ' me and ' saw my ' works.

EASTER ANTHEM

ANON

9

EASTER DAY

*At Morning Prayer, instead of the Psalm, O come, let us sing, etc.,
these Anthems shall be sung or said.*

1 CHRIST our passover is ' sacrificed ' for us : therefore ' let us '
keep the ' feast;

2 Not with the old leaven, nor with the leaven of ' malice and '
wickedness : but with the unleavened bread of sin'ceri'ty and '
truth.   *1 Cor. v. 7.*

3 Christ being raised from the dead ' dieth no ' more : death hath no '
more do'minion ' over him.

4 For in that he died, he died unto ' sin ' once : but in that he liveth,
he ' liveth ' unto ' God.

5 Likewise reckon ye also yourselves to be dead indeed ' unto ' sin :
but alive unto God through ' Jesus ' Christ our ' Lord.
Rom. vi. 9.

6 Christ is ' risen from the ' dead : and become the ' first-fruits of '
them that ' slept.

7 For since by ' man came ' death : by man came also the resur'rection '
of the ' dead.

8 For as in Adam ' all ' die : even so in Christ shall ' all be ' made a-'
live.   *1 Cor. xv. 20.*

Glory be to the Father, and ' to the ' Son : and ' to the ' Holy ' Ghost;

As it was in the beginning, is now and ' ever ' shall be : world without '
end. ' A'men.

TE DEUM LAUDAMUS

SET A

TRENT

SET B

E. J. HOPKINS

1 WE praise ' thee O ' God : we acknowledge ' thee to ' be the ' Lord

2 All the earth doth ' worship ' thee : the ' Father ' ever'lasting.

3 To thee all Angels ' cry a'loud : the Heavens and ' all the Powers there'in.

4 To thee ' Cherubin and ' Seraphin : con'tinual'ly do ' cry,

5 Holy ' Holy ' Holy : Lord ' God of ' Saba'oth;

† 6 Heaven and ' earth are ' full : of the ' Majesty ' of thy ' Glory.

7 The glorious company of the Apostles ' praise ' thee : the goodly fellowship of the ' Prophets ' praise ' thee :

8 The noble ' army of ' Martyrs : praise ' — ' — ' thee.

9 The holy Church throughout all the world doth ac'knowledge thee : the Father ' of an ' infinite ' Majesty,

10 Thine honourable true and ' only ' Son : also the ' Holy ' Ghost the Comforter.

† This verse may be sung without any break at the colon.

TE DEUM LAUDAMUS

11 Thou art the King of ' Glory O ' Christ : thou art the ever'lasting '
Son of the ' Father.

12 When thou tookest upon thee to de'liver ' man : thou didst not
ab'hor the ' Virgin's ' womb.

2nd 13 When thou hadst overcome the ' sharpness of ' death : thou didst
Part   open the Kingdom of ' Heaven to ' all be'lievers.

14 Thou sittest at the right ' hand of ' God : in the ' Glory ' of the '
Father.

   * 15 We be'lieve that ' thou ' shalt ' come : to ' be our ' judge.

16 We therefore pray thee ' help thy ' servants : whom thou hast
redeemed ' with thy ' precious ' blood.

17 Make them to be numbered ' with thy ' Saints : in ' glory '
ever'lasting.

---

15 We believe that ' thou shalt ' come : to ' be ' our ' judge.

TE DEUM LAUDAMUS

SET A   H. ALDRICH   SET B   R. FARRANT

12   15

18 O Lord save thy people and ' bless thine ' heritage : govern them and ' lift them ' up for ' ever.

19 Day by day we ' magnify ' thee : and we worship thy Name ' ever ' world without ' end.

20 Vouch'safe O ' Lord : to keep us this ' day with'out ' sin.

21 O Lord have ' mercy up'on us : have ' mer'cy up'on us.

22 O Lord let thy mercy ' lighten up'on us : as our ' trust is ' in ' thee.

23 O Lord in thee ' have I ' trusted : let me ' never ' be con'founded.

TE DEUM LAUDAMUS

SET C

J. DAVY

16

SET D

W. RUSSELL

19

1 WE praise ' thee O ' God : we acknowledge ' thee to ' be the ' Lord.

2 All the earth doth ' worship ' thee : the ' Father ' ever'lasting.

3 To thee all Angels ' cry a'loud : the Heavens and ' all the ' Powers there'in.

4 To thee ' Cherubin and ' Seraphin : con'tinual'ly do ' cry,

5 Holy ' Holy ' Holy : Lord ' God of ' Saba'oth;

† 6 Heaven and ' earth are ' full : of the ' Majesty ' of thy ' Glory.

7 The glorious company of the Apostles ' praise ' thee : the goodly fellowship of the ' Prophets ' praise ' thee :

8 The noble ' army of ' Martyrs : praise ' — ' — ' thee.

9 The holy Church throughout all the world doth ac'knowledge ' thee : the Father ' of an ' infinite ' Majesty,

10 Thine honourable true and ' only ' Son : also the ' Holy ' Ghost the ' Comforter.

---

† *This verse may be sung without any break at the colon.*

TE DEUM LAUDAMUS

SET C

R. COOKE

17

SET D

H. SMART

20

11 Thou art the King of ' Glory O ' Christ : thou art the ever'lasting ' Son of the ' Father.

12 When thou tookest upon thee to de'liver ' man : thou didst not ab'hor the ' Virgin's ' womb.

2nd Part 13 When thou hadst overcome the ' sharpness of ' death : thou didst open the Kingdom of ' Heaven to ' all be'lievers.

14 Thou sittest at the right ' hand of ' God : in the ' Glory ' of the ' Father.

* 15 We be'lieve that ' thou ' shalt ' come : to ' be our ' judge.

16 We therefore pray thee ' help thy ' servants : whom thou hast redeemed ' with thy ' precious ' blood.

17 Make them to be numbered ' with thy ' Saints : in ' glory ' ever'lasting.

15 We believe that ' thou shalt ' come : to ' be ' our ' judge.

TE DEUM LAUDAMUS

18 O Lord save thy people and ' bless thine ' heritage : govern them and '
lift them ' up for ' ever.

19 Day by day we ' magnify ' thee : and we worship thy Name ' ever '
world without ' end.

20 Vouch'safe O ' Lord : to keep us this ' day with'out ' sin.

21 O Lord have ' mercy up'on us : have ' mer'cy up'on us.

22 O Lord let thy mercy ' lighten up'on us : as our ' trust is ' in ' thee.

23 O Lord in thee ' have I ' trusted : let me ' never ' be con'founded.

Or this Canticle
BENEDICITE, OMNIA OPERA

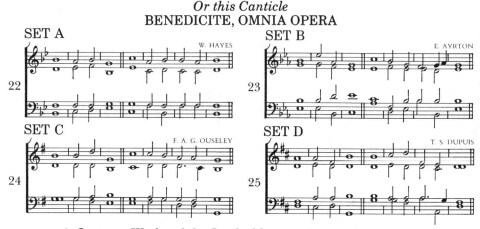

1 O ALL ye Works of the Lord ' bless ye the ' Lord : praise him and '
magnify ' him for ' ever.

2 O ye Angels of the Lord ' bless ye the ' Lord : praise him and '
magnify ' him for ' ever.

3 O ye Heavens ' bless ye the ' Lord : praise him and ' magnify '
him for ' ever.

4 O ye Waters that be above the Firmament ' bless ye the ' Lord :
praise him and ' magnify ' him for ' ever.

5 O all ye Powers of the Lord ' bless ye the ' Lord : praise him and '
magnify ' him for ' ever.

6 O ye Sun and Moon ' bless ye the ' Lord : praise him and ' magnify '
him for ' ever.

7 O ye Stars of Heaven ' bless ye the ' Lord : praise him and ' magnify '
him for ' ever.

8 O ye Showers and Dew ' bless ye the ' Lord : praise him and '
magnify ' him for ' ever.

9 O ye Winds of God ' bless ye the ' Lord : praise him and ' magnify '
him for ' ever.

10 O ye Fire and Heat ' bless ye the ' Lord : praise him and ' magnify '
him for ' ever.

11 O ye Winter and Summer ' bless ye the ' Lord : praise him and '
magnify ' him for ' ever.

12 O ye Dews and Frosts ' bless ye the ' Lord : praise him and '
magnify ' him for ' ever.

13 O ye Frost and Cold ' bless ye the ' Lord : praise him and ' magnify '
him for ' ever.

14 O ye Ice and Snow ' bless ye the ' Lord : praise him and ' magnify ' him for ' ever.

15 O ye Nights and Days ' bless ye the ' Lord : praise him and ' magnify ' him for ' ever.

16 O ye Light and Darkness ' bless ye the ' Lord : praise him and ' magnify ' him for ' ever.

17 O ye Lightnings and Clouds ' bless ye the ' Lord : praise him and ' magnify ' him for ' ever.

18 O let the Earth ' bless the ' Lord : yea let it praise him and ' magnify ' him for ' ever.

19 O ye Mountains and Hills ' bless ye the ' Lord : praise him and ' magnify ' him for ' ever.

20 O all ye Green Things upon the Earth ' bless ye the ' Lord : praise him and ' magnify ' him for ' ever.

21 O ye Wells ' bless ye the ' Lord : praise him and ' magnify ' him for ' ever.

22 O ye Seas and Floods ' bless ye the ' Lord : praise him and ' magnify ' him for ' ever.

23 O ye Whales and all that move in the Waters ' bless ye the ' Lord : praise him and ' magnify ' him for ' ever.

24 O all ye Fowls of the Air ' bless ye the ' Lord : praise him and ' magnify ' him for ' ever.

25 O all ye Beasts and Cattle ' bless ye the ' Lord : praise him and ' magnify ' him for ' ever.

26 O ye Children of Men ' bless ye the ' Lord : praise him and ' magnify ' him for ' ever.

27 O let Israel ' bless the ' Lord : praise him and ' magnify ' him for ' ever.

28 O ye Priests of the Lord ' bless ye the ' Lord : praise him and ' magnify ' him for ' ever.

29 O ye Servants of the Lord ' bless ye the ' Lord : praise him and ' magnify ' him for ' ever.

30 O ye Spirits and Souls of the Righteous ' bless ye the ' Lord : praise him and ' magnify ' him for ' ever.

31 O ye holy and humble Men of heart ' bless ye the ' Lord : praise him and ' magnify ' him for ' ever.

32 O Ananias Azarias and Misael ' bless ye the ' Lord : praise him and ' magnify ' him for ' ever.

Glory be to the Father, and ' to the ' Son : and ' to the ' Holy ' Ghost;

As it was in the beginning, is now and ' ever ' shall be : world without ' end.' A'men.

BENEDICTUS   St Luke i 68

SET A

H. SKEATS

26

SET B

R. LANGDON

27

SET C

J. LEMON

28

SET D

E. EDWARDS

29

1 BLESSED be the Lord ' God of ' Israel : for he hath ' visited · and re-' deemed his ' people;

2 And hath raised up a mighty sal'vation ' for us : in the ' house of his ' servant ' David;

3 As he spake by the mouth of his ' holy ' Prophets : which have been ' since the ' world be'gan;

4 That we should be saved ' from our ' enemies : and from the ' hands of ' all that ' hate us;

5 To perform the mercy promised ' to our ' forefathers : and to re-' member his ' holy ' Covenant;

* 6 To per'form the ' oath : which he ' sware to our ' fore · father ' Abraham;

* 7 That he would give us, that we being delivered out of the ' hand of our ' enemies : might ' serve him with'out ' fear;

8 In holiness and ' righteousness be'fore him : all the ' days of ' our ' life.

9 And thou Child shalt be called the ' Prophet of the ' Highest : for thou shalt go before the face of the Lord ' to pre'pare his ' ways;

10 To give knowledge of salvation ' unto his ' people : for the re'mission ' of their ' sins,

11 Through the tender mercy of ' our ' God : whereby the day-spring ' from on ' high hath ' visited us;

12 To give light to them that sit in darkness, and in the ' shadow of ' death : and to guide our feet ' into the ' way of ' peace.

Glory be to the Father, and ' to the ' Son : and ' to the ' Holy ' Ghost;

As it was in the beginning, is now and ' ever ' shall be : world without ' end. ' A'men.

---

6 To perform the oath which he sware to our ' fore · father ' Abraham : that ' he would ' give ' us;

7 That we being delivered out of the ' hand of our ' enemies : might ' serve him with'out ' fear;

MAGNIFICAT   St Luke i

SET A

SET B

SET C

SET D

MAGNIFICAT   St Luke i

1 My soul doth ' magnify the ' Lord : and my spirit hath re'joiced in ' God my ' Saviour.

2 For he ' hath re'garded : the ' lowliness ' of his ' handmaiden.

3 For be'hold from ' henceforth : all gene'rations shall ' call me ' blessed.

4 For he that is mighty hath ' magnified ' me : and ' holy ' is his ' Name.

5 And his mercy is on ' them that ' fear him : through'out all ' gene'rations.

6 He hath shew-ed ' strength with his ' arm : he hath scattered the proud, in the imagi'nation ' of their ' hearts.

7 He hath put down the mighty ' from their ' seat : and hath ex-' alted the ' humble and ' meek.

8 He hath fill-ed the hungry with ' good ' things : and the rich he ' hath sent ' empty a'way.

9 He re'membering his ' mercy : hath ' holpen his ' servant ' Israel.

10 As he promised ' to our ' forefathers : Abraham ' and his ' seed for ' ever.

Glory be to the Father, and ' to the ' Son : and ' to the ' Holy ' Ghost;

As it was in the beginning, is now and ' ever ' shall be : world without ' end.' A'men.

NUNC DIMITTIS   St Luke ii 29

SET A   H. BAKER

SET B   W. DYCE

34   35

SET C   G. A. MACFARREN

SET D   G. J. ELVEY

36   37

1 LORD now lettest thou thy servant de'part in ' peace : ac'cording ' to thy ' word.

2 For mine eyes have ' seen thy sal'vation : which thou hast prepared before the ' face of ' all ' people.

3 To be a light to ' lighten the ' Gentiles : and to be the ' glory · of thy ' people ' Israel.

Glory be to the Father, and ' to the ' Son : and ' to the ' Holy ' Ghost;

As it was in the beginning, is now and ' ever ' shall be : world without ' end.' A'men.

The Psalms of David

DAY 1 MORNING
PSALM 1

P. FUSSELL

38

BLESSED is the man that hath not walked in the counsel of the ungodly,
    nor stood in the ' way of ' sinners : and hath not ' sat · in the '
    seat of the ' scornful.

2 But his delight is in the ' law of the ' Lord : and in his law will he
    exercise him'self ' day and ' night.

3 And he shall be like a tree planted by the ' water'side : that will
    bring forth his ' fruit in ' due ' season.

4 His leaf also ' shall not ' wither : and look, whatsoever he ' doeth '
    it shall ' prosper.

5 As for the ungodly, it is not ' so with ' them : but they are like the
    chaff, which the wind scattereth a'way · from the ' face of the '
    earth.

6 Therefore the ungodly shall not be able to ' stand · in the '
    judgement : neither the sinners in the congre'gation ' of the '
    righteous.

2nd 7 But the Lord knoweth the ' way · of the ' righteous : and the '
Part   way of · the un'godly shall ' perish.

PSALM 2

W. TURNER

39

Single Chant

WHY do the heathen so furiously ' rage to'gether : and why do the
    people i'magine a ' vain ' thing?

2 The kings of the earth stand up, and the rulers take ' counsel to-'
    gether : against the ' Lord and a'gainst his A'nointed.

3 Let us break their ' bonds a'sunder : and cast a'way their ' cords '
    from us.

23

W. TURNER

39

4 He that dwelleth in heaven shall ' laugh them to ' scorn : the Lord shall ' have them ' in de'rision.

5 Then shall he speak unto them ' in his ' wrath : and vex them ' in his ' sore dis'pleasure.

6 Yet have I ' set my ' King : upon my ' holy ' hill of ' Sion.

7 I will preach the law, whereof the Lord hath ' said unto ' me : Thou art my Son, this day have ' I be'gotten ' thee.

8 Desire of me, and I shall give thee the heathen for ' thine in'heritance : and the utmost parts of the ' earth for ' thy pos'session.

9 Thou shalt bruise them with a ' rod of ' iron : and break them in pieces ' like a ' potter's ' vessel.

10 Be wise now therefore ' O ye ' kings : be learned, ye that are ' judges ' of the ' earth.

11 Serve the ' Lord in ' fear : and re'joice unto ' him with ' reverence.

12 Kiss the Son lest he be angry, and so ye perish from the ' right ' way : if his wrath be kindled (yea but a little), blessed are all they that ' put their ' trust in ' him.

PSALM 3

H. J. GAUNTLETT

40

p   LORD, how are they in'creased that ' trouble me : many are ' they that ' rise a'gainst me.

2 Many one there be that ' say of my ' soul : There is no help ' for him ' in his ' God.

3 But thou O Lord art ' my de'fender : thou art my worship, and the '
   lifter ' up of my ' head.

4 I did call upon the Lord ' with my ' voice : and he heard me '
   out of his ' holy ' hill.

5 I laid me down and slept, and rose ' up a'gain : for the ' Lord sus-'
   tain-ed ' me.

6 I will not be afraid for ten ' thousands · of the ' people : that have
   set themselves a'gainst me ' round a'bout.

f   7 Up Lord and help me ' O my ' God : for thou smitest all mine
     enemies upon the cheek-bone, thou hast broken the ' teeth of '
     the un'godly.

8 Salvation belongeth ' unto the ' Lord : and thy blessing ' is up-'
   on thy ' people.

PSALM 4

J. SOAPER

41

HEAR me when I call O ' God of my ' righteousness : thou hast set me
   at liberty when I was in trouble, have mercy upon me and '
   hearken ' unto my ' prayer.

2 O ye sons of men, how long will ye blas'pheme mine ' honour : and
   have such pleasure in vanity and ' seek ' after ' leasing?

3 Know this also, that the Lord hath chosen to himself the '
   man that is ' godly : when I call upon the ' Lord ' he will '
   hear me.

4 Stand in ' awe and ' sin not : commune with your own heart, and in
   your ' chamber ' and be ' still.

5 Offer the ' sacrifice of ' righteousness : and ' put your ' trust · in the '
   Lord.

6 There be ' many that ' say : Who will ' shew us ' any ' good?

7 Lord ' lift thou ' up : the light of thy ' counte'nance up'on us.

8 Thou hast put gladness ' in my ' heart : since the time that their
   corn and ' wine and ' oil in'creased.

2nd   9 I will lay me down in peace and ' take my ' rest : for it is thou Lord
Part   only that ' makest me ' dwell in ' safety.

25

PSALM 5

WOODS

42

PONDER my ' words O ' Lord : con'sider my ' medi'tation.

2 O hearken thou unto the voice of my calling, my ' King and my '
God : for unto ' thee will I ' make my ' prayer.

3 My voice shalt thou hear be'times O ' Lord : early in the morning
will I direct my prayer unto thee ' and will ' look ' up.

4 For thou art the God that hast no ' pleasure in ' wickedness :
neither shall any ' evil ' dwell with ' thee.

5 Such as be foolish shall not ' stand in thy ' sight : for thou '
hatest all ' them that work ' vanity.

6 Thou shalt destroy ' them that speak ' leasing : the Lord will abhor
both the bloodthirsty ' and de'ceitful ' man.

2nd
Part
7 But as for me I will come into thine house, even upon the multitude
of ' thy ' mercy : and in thy fear will I worship ' toward thy ' holy '
temple.

8 Lead me O Lord in thy righteousness, be'cause of mine ' enemies :
make thy way ' plain be'fore my ' face.

9 For there is no faithfulness ' in his ' mouth : their inward '
parts are ' very ' wickedness.

10 Their throat is an ' open ' sepulchre : they ' flatter ' with their '
tongue.

11 Destroy thou them O God, let them perish through their own
i'magi'nations : cast them out in the multitude of their ungodliness, for ' they have re'belled a'gainst thee.

12 And let all them that put their trust in ' thee re'joice : they shall
ever be giving of thanks because thou defendest them, they that
love thy Name ' shall be ' joyful in ' thee;

13 For thou Lord wilt give thy blessing ' unto the ' righteous : and
with thy favourable kindness wilt thou de'fend him ' as with a '
shield.

DAY 1 EVENING

PSALM 6

43

p   O LORD rebuke me not in thine ' indig'nation : neither ' chasten · me in ' thy dis'pleasure.

2 Have mercy upon me O Lord for ' I am ' weak : O Lord heal me ' for my ' bones are ' vexed.

3 My soul also is ' sore ' troubled : but ' Lord how ' long · wilt thou ' punish me?

4 Turn thee O Lord and de'liver my ' soul : O save me ' for thy ' mercy's ' sake.

5 For in death ' no man re'membereth thee : and who will ' give thee ' thanks in the ' pit?

6 I am weary of my groaning, every night ' wash I my ' bed : and ' water my ' couch with my ' tears.

2nd   7 My beauty is gone for ' very ' trouble : and worn away be'cause of '
Part   all mine ' enemies.

44

f   8 Away from me all ' ye that work ' vanity : for the Lord hath ' heard the ' voice of my ' weeping.

9 The Lord hath ' heard my pe'tition : the ' Lord will re'ceive my ' prayer.

2nd 10 All mine enemies shall be confounded and ' sore ' vexed : they shall
Part   be turned back and ' put to ' shame ' suddenly.

PSALM 7

E. J. HOPKINS

45

p   O LORD my God, in thee have I ' put my ' trust : save me from all them that persecute me ' and de'liver ' me;

2 Lest he devour my soul like a lion and ' tear it in ' pieces : while ' there is ' none to ' help.

3 O Lord my God if I have done ' any such ' thing : or if there be any ' wickedness ' in my ' hands;

4 If I have rewarded evil unto him that dealt ' friendly ' with me : yea I have delivered him that with'out · any ' cause is mine ' enemy;

5 Then let mine enemy persecute my ' soul and ' take me : yea let him tread my life down upon the earth, and lay mine ' honour ' in the ' dust.

6 Stand up O Lord in thy wrath and lift up thyself, because of the indignation ' of mine ' enemies : arise up for me in the ' judgement that ' thou hast com'manded.

7 And so shall the congregation of the people ' come a'bout thee : for their sakes therefore lift ' up thy'self a'gain.

8 The Lord shall judge the people, give sentence with ' me O ' Lord : according to my righteousness, and according to the ' innocency ' that is ' in me.

9 O let the wickedness of the ungodly ' come to an ' end : but ' guide ' thou the ' just.

10 For the ' righteous ' God : trieth the ' very ' hearts and ' reins.

f   11 My help ' cometh of ' God : who preserveth ' them that are ' true of ' heart.

12 God is a righteous Judge ' strong and ' patient : and God is pro'vok-ed' every ' day.

13 If a man will not turn he will ' whet his ' sword : he hath bent his ' bow and ' made it ' ready.

14 He hath prepared for him the ' instruments of ' death : he ordaineth his ' arrows a'gainst the ' persecutors.

15 Behold he ' travaileth with ' mischief : he hath conceived sorrow and ' brought ' forth un'godliness.

16 He hath graven and dig-ged ' up a ' pit : and is fallen himself into the destruction ' that he ' made for ' other.

17 For his travail shall come upon his ' own ' head : and his wickedness shall ' fall on his ' own ' pate.

18 I will give thanks unto the Lord, ac'cording · to his ' righteousness : and I will praise the ' Name · of the ' Lord most ' High.

PSALM 8

F. A. G. OUSELEY

46

Single Chant

Unison O LORD our Governor, how excellent is thy Name in ' all the ' world : thou that hast set thy ' glory a'bove the ' heavens!

2 Out of the mouth of very babes and sucklings hast thou ordained strength, be'cause of thine ' enemies : that thou mightest still the ' enemy ' and the a'venger.

3 For I will consider thy heavens, even the ' works of thy ' fingers : the moon and the stars ' which thou ' hast or'dained.

4 What is man, that thou art ' mindful of ' him : and the son of man, that ' thou ' visitest ' him?

5 Thou madest him lower ' than the ' angels : to ' crown him with ' glory and ' worship.

6 Thou makest him to have dominion of the ' works of thy ' hands : and thou hast put all things in sub'jection ' under his ' feet;

7 All ' sheep and ' oxen : yea and the ' beasts ' of the ' field;

8 The fowls of the air and the ' fishes   of the ' sea : and whatsoever walketh ' through the ' paths of the ' seas.

Unison 9 O ' Lord our ' Governor : how excellent is thy ' Name in ' all the ' world!

29

DAY 2   MORNING
PSALM 9

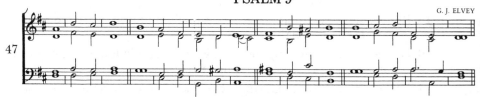

G. J. ELVEY

47

I WILL give thanks unto thee O Lord with my ' whole ' heart : I will speak of ' all thy ' marvellous ' works.

2 I will be glad and re'joice in ' thee : yea my songs will I make of thy ' Name O ' thou most ' Highest.

3 While mine enemies are ' driven ' back : they shall fall and ' perish ' at thy ' presence.

4 For thou hast maintained my ' right and my ' cause : thou art set in the ' throne that ' judgest ' right.

5 Thou hast rebuked the heathen, and de'stroyed the un'godly : thou hast put out their ' name for ' ever and ' ever.

6 O thou enemy, destructions are come to a per'petual ' end : even as the cities which thou hast destroyed, their me'morial is ' perish-ed ' with them.

7 But the Lord shall en'dure for ' ever : he hath also pre'pared his ' seat for ' judgement.

8 For he shall judge the ' world in ' righteousness : and minister true ' judgement ' unto the ' people.

9 The Lord also will be a defence ' for the op'pressed : even a refuge in ' due ' time of ' trouble.

10 And they that know thy Name will put their ' trust in ' thee : for thou Lord hast never ' fail-ed ' them that ' seek thee.

11 O praise the Lord which ' dwelleth in ' Sion : shew the ' people ' of his ' doings.

12 For when he maketh inquisition for blood, he re'membereth ' them : and forgetteth not the com'plaint ' of the ' poor.

13 Have mercy upon me O Lord, consider the trouble which I suffer of ' them that ' hate me : thou that liftest me up ' from the ' gates of ' death.

14 That I may shew all thy praises within the ports of the ' daughter of ' Sion : I will re'joice in ' thy sal'vation.

15 The heathen are sunk down in the pit ' that they ' made : in the same net which they hid privily ' is their ' foot ' taken.

16 The Lord is known to ' execute ' judgement : the ungodly is trapped in the ' work of his ' own ' hands.

17 The wicked shall be turned ' into ' hell : and all the people ' that for'get ' God.

18 For the poor shall not alway ' be for'gotten : the patient abiding of the meek ' shall not ' perish for ' ever.

19 Up Lord, and let not man have the ' upper ' hand : let the heathen be ' judg-ed ' in thy ' sight.

20 Put them in ' fear O ' Lord : that the heathen may know them-' selves to ' be but ' men.

PSALM 10

p WHY standest thou so far ' off O ' Lord : and hidest thy face in the ' needful ' time of ' trouble?

2 The ungodly for his own lust doth ' persecute the ' poor : let them be taken in the crafty wiliness ' that they ' have i'magined.

3 For the ungodly hath made boast of his own ' heart's de'sire : and speaketh good of the covetous ' whom ' God ab'horreth.

4 The ungodly is so proud that he careth ' not for ' God : neither is ' God in ' all his ' thoughts.

5 His ways are ' alway ' grievous : thy judgements are far above out of his sight, and therefore de'fieth he ' all his ' enemies.

6 For he hath said in his heart, Tush I shall never be ' cast ' down : there shall no harm ' happen ' unto ' me.

7 His mouth is full of cursing de'ceit and ' fraud : under his ' tongue is un'godliness and ' vanity.

8 He sitteth lurking in the thievish ' corners · of the ' streets : and privily in his lurking dens doth he murder the innocent, his eyes are ' set a'gainst the ' poor.

31

9 For he lieth waiting secretly, even as a lion lurketh he ' in his '
den : that ' he may ' ravish the ' poor.

10 He doth ' ravish the ' poor : when he ' getteth him ' into his ' net.

11 He falleth down and ' humbleth him'self : that the congregation of
the poor may fall ' into the ' hands of his ' captains.

12 He hath said in his heart, Tush ' God hath for'gotten : he hideth
away his face and ' he will ' never ' see it.

f 13 Arise O Lord God and lift ' up thine ' hand : for'get ' not the ' poor.

14 Wherefore should the wicked blas'pheme ' God : while he doth say
in his heart, Tush, ' thou God ' carest not ' for it.

15 Surely ' thou hast ' seen it : for thou be'holdest un'godliness and '
wrong.

16 That thou mayest take the matter ' into thy ' hand : the poor
committeth himself unto thee, for thou art the ' helper ' of the '
friendless.

17 Break thou the power of the ungodly ' and ma'licious : take away
his ungodliness and ' thou shalt ' find ' none.

18 The Lord is King for ' ever and ' ever : and the heathen are '
perished ' out of the ' land.

19 Lord thou hast heard the de'sire of the ' poor : thou preparest their
heart, and thine ear ' hearkeneth ' there'to;

20 To help the fatherless and poor ' unto their ' right : that the man of
the earth be no ' more ex'alted a'gainst them.

PSALM 11

50

IN the Lord put ' I my ' trust : how say ye then to my soul, that she should flee as a ' bird ' unto the ' hill?

2 For lo the ungodly bend their bow, and make ready their arrows with'in the ' quiver : that they may privily shoot at them ' which are ' true of ' heart.

2nd Part 3 For the foundations will be ' cast ' down : and ' what hath the ' righteous ' done?

4 The Lord is in his ' holy ' temple : the Lord's ' seat ' is in ' heaven.

5 His eyes con'sider the ' poor : and his eyelids ' try the ' children of ' men.

6 The Lord al'loweth the ' righteous : but the ungodly and him that delighteth in wickedness ' doth his ' soul ab'hor.

7 Upon the ungodly he shall rain snares, fire and brimstone ' storm and ' tempest : this shall ' be their ' portion to ' drink.

2nd Part 8 For the righteous Lord ' loveth ' righteousness : his countenance will be'hold the ' thing that is ' just.

DAY 2   EVENING
PSALM 12

51

HELP me Lord for there is not one ' godly man ' left : for the faithful are minished from a'mong the ' children of ' men.

2 They talk of vanity every one ' with his ' neighbour : they do but flatter with their lips, and dissemble ' in their ' double ' heart.

3 The Lord shall root out all de'ceitful ' lips : and the tongue that ' speaketh ' proud ' things;

4 Which have said, With our tongue will ' we pre'vail : we are they that ought to speak, ' who is ' lord over ' us?

33

L. FLINTOFT

51

5 Now for the comfortless trouble's sake ' of the ' needy : and because of the deep ' sighing ' of the ' poor,

6 I will up ' saith the ' Lord : and will help every one from him that swelleth against him ' and will ' set him at ' rest.

7 The words of the ' Lord are ' pure words : even as the silver which from the earth is tried, and purified ' seven times ' in the ' fire.

8 Thou shalt ' keep them O ' Lord : thou shalt preserve him from ' this · gene'ration for ' ever.

2nd Part   9 The ungodly walk on ' every ' side : when they are exalted, the children of ' men are ' put to re'buke.

PSALM 13

G. WOODWARD

52

p   How long wilt thou forget me O ' Lord for ' ever : how long wilt thou ' hide thy ' face ' from me?

2 How long shall I seek counsel in my soul, and be so vexed ' in my ' heart : how long shall mine ' enemies ' triumph ' over me?

3 Consider and hear me O ' Lord my ' God : lighten mine eyes that I ' sleep ' not in ' death.

4 Lest mine enemy say, I have pre'vailed a'gainst him : for if I be cast down, they that trouble me ' will re'joice ' at it.

f   5 But my trust is ' in thy ' mercy : and my heart is ' joyful in ' thy sal'vation.

6 I will sing of the Lord, because he hath dealt so ' lovingly ' with me : yea I will praise the ' Name of the ' Lord most ' Highest.

PSALM 14

or

THE fool hath said ' in his ' heart : There ' is ' no ' God.

2 They are corrupt, and become abominable ' in their ' doings : there is none that doeth ' good ' no not ' one.

3 The Lord looked down from heaven upon the ' children of ' men : to see if there were any that would understand and ' seek ' after ' God.

4 But they are all gone out of the way, they are altogether be-' come a'bominable : there is none that doeth ' good ' no not ' one.

[5 Their throat is an open sepulchre, with their tongues have ' they de'ceived : the poison of ' asps is ' under their ' lips.

6 Their mouth is full of ' cursing and ' bitterness : their feet are ' swift to ' shed ' blood.

7 Destruction and unhappiness is in their ways, and the way of peace have ' they not ' known : there is no fear of ' God be'fore their ' eyes.]

8 Have they no knowledge, that they are all such ' workers of ' mischief : eating up my people as it were bread, and ' call not up'on the ' Lord?

9 There were they brought in great fear, even where ' no fear ' was : for God is in the gene'ration ' of the ' righteous.

10 As for you, ye have made a mock at the counsel ' of the ' poor : because he ' putteth his ' trust in the ' Lord.

2nd Part 11 Who shall give salvation unto Israel ' out of ' Sion? : When the Lord turneth the captivity of his people, then shall Jacob rejoice and ' Israel ' shall be ' glad.

35

DAY 3   MORNING
PSALM 15

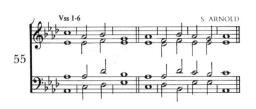

Single Chant

LORD who shall ' dwell in thy ' tabernacle : or who shall rest up'on thy holy ' hill?

2 Even he that leadeth an ' uncorrupt ' life : and doeth the thing which is right, and speaketh the ' truth ' from his ' heart.

3 He that hath used no deceit in his tongue, nor done evil ' to his neighbour : and ' hath not ' slandered his ' neighbour.

4 He that setteth not by himself, but is lowly in his ' own ' eyes : and maketh much of ' them that ' fear the ' Lord.

5 He that sweareth unto his neighbour, and disap'pointeth him ' not though it ' were to his ' own ' hindrance.

6 He that hath not given his ' money · upon ' usury : nor taken re'ward a'gainst the ' innocent.

Unison
½   7 Whoso doeth these ' things : shall ' never ' fall.

PSALM 16

PRESERVE ' me O ' God : for in thee ' have I ' put my ' trust.

2 O my soul thou hast said ' unto the ' Lord : Thou art my God, my goods are ' nothing ' unto ' thee.

3 All my delight is upon the saints that are ' in the ' earth : and upon such as ex'cel in ' virtue.

4 But they that run after an'other ' god : shall ' have ' great ' trouble

Ps. 15. vs. 7 Whoso ' doeth these ' things : shall ' ne'ver ' fall.

5 Their drink-offerings of blood will ' I not ' offer : neither make mention of their ' names with'in my ' lips.

6 The Lord himself is the portion of mine inheritance and ' of my ' cup : thou ' shalt main'tain my ' lot.

7 The lot is fallen unto me in a ' fair ' ground : yea I ' have a ' goodly ' heritage.

8 I will thank the Lord for ' giving me ' warning : my reins also chasten me ' in the ' night'season.

9 I have set God ' always be'fore me : for he is on my right hand ' therefore I ' shall not ' fall.

10 Wherefore my heart was glad and my ' glory re'joiced : my flesh ' also shall ' rest in ' hope.

11 For why?, thou shalt not leave my ' soul in ' hell : neither shalt thou suffer thy ' Holy One to ' see cor'ruption.

12 Thou shalt shew me the path of life, in thy presence is the ' fulness of ' joy : and at thy right hand there is ' pleasure for ' ever'more.

PSALM 17

J. TURLE

57

HEAR the right O Lord, consider ' my com'plaint : and hearken unto my prayer that goeth not ' out of ' feign-ed ' lips.

2 Let my sentence come forth ' from thy ' presence : and let thine eyes look up'on the ' thing that is ' equal.

3 Thou hast proved and visited mine heart in the night-season, thou hast tried me and shalt find no ' wickedness ' in me : for I am utterly purposed that my ' mouth shall ' not of'fend.

4 Because of men's works, that are done against the ' words of thy ' lips : I have kept me from the ' ways of ' the de'stroyer.

Verse overleaf

J. TURLE

57

* 5 O hold thou up my ' goings ' in thy ' paths : ' that my ' footsteps ' slip not.

6 I have called upon thee O God for ' thou shalt ' hear me : incline thine ear to me and ' hearken ' unto my ' words.

7 Shew thy marvellous loving-kindness, thou that art the Saviour of them which put their ' trust in ' thee : from such as re'sist thy ' right ' hand.

8 Keep me as the ' apple · of an ' eye : hide me under the ' shadow ' of thy ' wings,

9 From the un'godly that ' trouble me : mine enemies compass me round about to ' take a'way my ' soul.

10 They are inclosed in their ' own ' fat : and their mouth ' speaketh ' proud ' things.

11 They lie waiting in our way on ' every ' side : turning their ' eyes ' down to the ' ground;

12 Like as a lion that is ' greedy · of his ' prey : and as it were a lion's whelp ' lurking in ' secret ' places.

13 Up Lord, disappoint him and ' cast him ' down : deliver my soul from the ungodly which ' is a ' sword of ' thine;

14 From the men of thy hand O Lord, from the men I say and from the ' evil ' world : which have their portion in this life, whose bellies thou fillest ' with thy ' hid ' treasure.

15 They have children at ' their de'sire : and leave the rest of their ' substance ' for their ' babes.

16 But as for me, I will behold thy ' presence in ' righteousness : and when I awake up after thy likeness ' I shall be ' satisfied ' with it.

Vs 5

O hold thou up my go - ings   in thy   paths: that   my   foot - steps   slip not.

5 O hold thou up my goings ' in thy ' paths : that my ' footsteps ' slip ' not.

DAY 3   EVENING
PSALM 18

58

*   I WILL love thee O ' Lord my ' strength : the Lord is my stony '
rock and ' my de'fence.

1a My Saviour my God and my might, in whom ' I will ' trust : my
buckler, the horn also of my sal'vation ' and my ' refuge.

*2nd
Part*

2 I will call upon the Lord which is ' worthy · to be ' praised : so shall '
I be ' safe from mine ' enemies.

3 The sorrows of ' death ' compassed me : and the overflowings of
un'godliness ' made me a'fraid.

4 The pains of hell ' came a'bout me : the snares of ' death ' over-'
took me.

5 In my trouble I will call up'on the ' Lord : and com'plain ' unto my '
God.

6 So shall he hear my voice out of his ' holy ' temple : and my
complaint shall come before him, it shall enter ' even ' into his '
ears.

7 The earth ' trembled and ' quaked : the very foundations also of the
hills shook, and were re'moved be'cause he was ' wroth.

8 There went a smoke out ' in his ' presence : and a consuming fire
out of his mouth, so that ' coals were ' kindled ' at it.

9 He bowed the heavens also and ' came ' down : and it was ' dark '
under his ' feet.

10 He rode upon the cherubins ' and did ' fly : he came flying up'on the '
wings of the ' wind.

11 He made darkness his ' secret ' place : his pavilion round about
him, with dark water and thick ' clouds to ' cover ' him.

12 At the brightness of his presence his ' clouds re'moved : hail-'
stones and ' coals of ' fire.

---

* I will love thee O Lord my strength; the Lord is my stony rock and ' my de'fence : my
Saviour my God and my might in whom I will trust, my buckler, the horn also of
my sal'vation ' and my ' refuge.

58

13 The Lord also thundered out of heaven, and the Highest ' gave his '
thunder : hail'stones and ' coals of ' fire.

14 He sent out his ' arrows and ' scattered them : he cast forth '
lightnings ' and de'stroyed them.

15 The springs of waters were seen, and the foundations of the round
world were discovered, at thy ' chiding O ' Lord : at the blasting
of the ' breath of ' thy dis'pleasure.

16 He shall send down from on ' high to ' fetch me : and shall take me '
out of ' many ' waters.

17 He shall deliver me from my strongest enemy, and from '
them which ' hate me : for they ' are too ' mighty ' for me.

18 They prevented me in the ' day of my ' trouble : but the ' Lord was '
my up'holder.

19 He brought me forth also into a ' place of ' liberty : he brought me
forth, even because he had a ' favour ' unto ' me.

20 The Lord shall reward me after my ' righteous ' dealing : according
to the cleanness of my hands ' shall he ' recompense ' me.

21 Because I have kept the ' ways of the ' Lord : and have not forsaken
my God ' as the ' wicked ' doth.

22 For I have an eye unto ' all his ' laws : and will not cast out '
his com'mandments ' from me.

23 I was also uncor'rupt be'fore him : and es'chewed mine ' own '
wickedness.

24 Therefore shall the Lord reward me after my ' righteous ' dealing :
and according unto the cleanness of my ' hands in ' his ' eyesight.

25 With the holy ' thou shalt be ' holy : and with a ' perfect man '
thou shalt be ' perfect.

26 With the clean ' thou shalt be ' clean : and with the ' froward '
thou shalt learn ' frowardness.

27 For thou shalt save the people that are ' in ad'versity : and shalt
bring down the ' high ' looks of the ' proud.

28 Thou also shalt ' light my ' candle : the Lord my God shall make
my ' darkness ' to be ' light.

29 For in thee I shall discomfit an ' host of ' men : and with the help of my God I shall ' leap ' over the ' wall.

30 The way of God is an unde'fil-ed ' way : the word of the Lord also is tried in the fire, he is the defender of all them that ' put their ' trust in ' him.

31 For who is ' God · but the ' Lord : or who hath any ' strength ex-' cept our ' God?

32 It is God that girdeth me with ' strength of ' war : and ' maketh my ' way ' perfect.

33 He maketh my ' feet like ' harts' feet : and ' setteth me ' up on ' high.

34 He teacheth mine ' hands to.' fight : and mine arms shall break ' even a ' bow of ' steel.

35 Thou hast given me the defence of ' thy sal'vation : thy right hand also shall hold me up, and thy loving cor'rection shall ' make me ' great.

36 Thou shalt make room enough under me ' for to ' go : that my ' footsteps ' shall not ' slide.

37 I will follow upon mine enemies and ' over'take them : neither will I turn again ' till I ' have de'stroyed them.

38 I will smite them that they shall not be ' able to ' stand : but ' fall ' under my ' feet.

39 Thou hast girded me with strength ' unto the ' battle : thou shalt throw ' down mine ' enemies ' under me.

40 Thou hast made mine enemies also to turn their ' backs up'on me : and I shall de'stroy ' them that ' hate me.

41 They shall cry, but there shall be ' none to ' help them : yea, even unto the Lord shall they cry ' but he ' shall not ' hear them.

42 I will beat them as small as the dust be'fore the ' wind : I will cast them ' out as the ' clay · in the ' streets.

41

43 Thou shalt deliver me from the ' strivings · of the ' people : and
thou shalt ' make me the ' head of the ' heathen.

*   44 A people ' whom I ' have ' not ' known : shall ' serve ' me.

45 As soon as they hear of me ' they shall o'bey me : but the strange
children ' shall dis'semble ' with me.

46 The strange ' children shall ' fail : and be a'fraid ' out of their '
prisons.

47 The Lord liveth, and blessed be my ' strong ' helper : and prais-ed
be the ' God of ' my sal'vation;

48 Even the God that seeth that I ' be a'venged : and subdueth the '
people ' unto ' me.

49 It is he that delivereth me from my cruel enemies, and setteth me
up a'bove mine ' adversaries : thou shalt rid me ' from the '
wicked ' man.

50 For this cause will I give thanks unto thee O Lord a'mong the '
Gentiles : and sing ' praises ' unto thy ' Name.

2nd   51 Great prosperity giveth he ' unto his ' King : and sheweth loving-
Part   kindness unto David his Anointed, and unto his ' seed for '
ever'more.

* *In a case like this these notes would of course be quite short.*

44 A people whom I ' have not ' known : shall ' serve ' — ' me.

DAY 4 MORNING

PSALM 19

THE heavens declare the ' glory of ' God : and the ' firmament '
sheweth his ' handy-work.

2 One day ' telleth an'other : and one night ' certi'fieth an'other.

3 There is neither ' speech nor ' language : but their ' voices are '
heard a'mong them.

4 Their sound is gone out into ' all ' lands : and their words ' into the '
ends of the ' world.

5 In them hath he set a tabernacle ' for the ' sun : which cometh forth
as a bridegroom out of his chamber, and rejoiceth as a ' giant to '
run his ' course.

6 It goeth forth from the uttermost part of the heaven, and runneth
about unto the end of ' it a'gain : and there is nothing hid '
from the ' heat there'of.

(Or the whole of Psalm 19 may be sung to chant 61)

7 The law of the Lord is an undefiled law con'verting the ' soul : the
testimony of the Lord is sure, and giveth ' wisdom ' unto the '
simple.

8 The statutes of the Lord are right and re'joice the ' heart : the
commandment of the Lord is pure, and giveth ' light ' unto the '
eyes.

9 The fear of the Lord is clean and en'dureth for ' ever : the
judgements of the Lord are true and ' righteous ' alto'gether.

10 More to be desired are they than gold, yea than ' much fine ' gold :
sweeter also than ' honey ' and the ' honey-comb.

(Or the whole of Psalm 19 may be sung to chant 61)

11 Moreover by them is thy ' servant ' taught : and in keeping of them '
there is ' great re'ward.

12 Who can tell how ' oft he of'fendeth : O cleanse thou me ' from my '
secret ' faults.

13 Keep thy servant also from presumptuous sins, lest they get the
do'minion ' over me : so shall I be undefiled and innocent '
from the ' great of'fence.

14 Let the words of my mouth and the meditation ' of my ' heart : be
alway ac'ceptable ' in thy ' sight,

½ 15 O Lord : my ' strength and ' my re'deemer.

Return to Chant 60 for Gloria

PSALM 20

62

THE Lord hear thee in the ' day of ' trouble : the Name of the ' God of '
Jacob de'fend thee;

2 Send thee help ' from the ' sanctuary : and ' strengthen thee '
out of ' Sion;

3 Remember ' all thy ' offerings : and ac'cept thy ' burnt ' sacrifice;

4 Grant thee thy ' heart's de'sire : and ful'fil ' all thy ' mind.

5 We will rejoice in thy salvation, and triumph in the Name of the '
Lord our ' God : the Lord per'form all ' thy pe'titions.

6 Now know I that the Lord helpeth his Anointed, and will hear him
from his ' holy ' heaven : even with the wholesome ' strength of '
his right ' hand.

15 O ' — ' Lord : my ' strength and ' my re'deemer.

7 Some put their trust in chariots and ' some in ' horses : but we will remember the ' Name of the ' Lord our ' God.

8 They are brought ' down and ' fallen : but we are ' risen and ' stand ' upright.

2nd Part 9 Save Lord and hear us O ' King of ' heaven : when we ' call up'on ' thee.

PSALM 21

J. GOSS

63

THE King shall rejoice in thy ' strength O ' Lord : exceeding glad shall he ' be of ' thy sal'vation.

2 Thou hast given him his ' heart's de'sire : and hast not de-' nied him the re'quest of his ' lips.

3 For thou shalt prevent him with the ' blessings of ' goodness : and shalt set a crown of pure ' gold up'on his ' head.

* 4 He asked life of thee, and thou ' gavest · him a ' long ' life : ' even for ' ever and " ever.

5 His honour is great in ' thy sal'vation : glory and great worship ' shalt thou ' lay up'on him.

6 For thou shalt give him ever'lasting fe'licity : and make him glad with the ' joy of ' thy ' countenance.

He asked life of thee, and thou gav-est him a long life: ev-en for ev-er and ever.

4 He asked life of thee, and thou gavest him a ' long ' life : even for ' ever ' and ' ever.

45

J. GOSS

7 And why?, because the King putteth his ' trust in the ' Lord : and in the mercy of the most Highest ' he shall ' not mis'carry.

8 All thine enemies shall ' feel thine ' hand : thy right hand shall ' find out ' them that ' hate thee.

9 Thou shalt make them like a fiery oven in ' time of thy ' wrath : the Lord shall destroy them in his displeasure, and the ' fire ' shall con'sume them.

10 Their fruit shalt thou root ' out of the ' earth : and their seed from a'mong the ' children of ' men.

11 For they intended ' mischief a'gainst thee : and imagined such a device as they are not ' able ' to per'form.

12 Therefore shalt thou ' put them to ' flight : and the strings of thy bow shalt thou make ' ready a'gainst the ' face of them.

2nd Part 13 Be thou exalted Lord in thine ' own ' strength : so will we ' sing and ' praise thy ' power.

DAY 4   EVENING

PSALM 22

S. WESLEY

p MY God, my God, look upon me, why hast ' thou for'saken me : and art so far from my health, and from the ' words of ' my com'plaint?

2 O my God I cry in the day-time ' but thou ' hearest not : and in the night-season ' also I ' take no ' rest.

3 And thou con'tinuest ' holy : O ' thou ' worship of ' Israel.

46

4 Our fathers ' hoped in ' thee : they trusted in thee ' and thou ' didst de'liver them.

5 They called upon thee ' and were ' holpen : they put their trust in thee ' and were ' not con'founded.

6 But as for me, I am a worm and ' no ' man : a very scorn of men and the ' outcast ' of the ' people.

7 All they that see me ' laugh me to ' scorn : they shoot out their lips and ' shake their ' heads ' saying,

8 He trusted in God that ' he would de'liver him : let him de-' liver him ' if he will ' have him.

9 But thou art he that took me out of my ' mother's ' womb : thou wast my hope, when I hang-ed yet up'on my ' mother's ' breasts.

10 I have been left unto thee ever since ' I was ' born : thou art my God ' even · from my ' mother's ' womb.

11 O go not from me, for trouble is ' hard at ' hand : and ' there is ' none to ' help me.

12 Many oxen are ' come a'bout me : fat bulls of Basan close me ' in on ' every ' side.

13 They gape upon me ' with their ' mouths : as it were a ' ramping · and a ' roaring ' lion.

14 I am poured out like water, and all my bones are ' out of ' joint : my heart also in the midst of my body is ' even like ' melting ' wax.

15 My strength is dried up like a potsherd, and my tongue ' cleaveth · to my ' gums : and thou shalt bring me ' into the ' dust of ' death.

16 For many dogs are ' come a'bout me : and the council of the wicked ' layeth ' siege a'gainst me.

17 They pierced my hands and my feet, I may tell ' all my ' bones : they stand ' staring and ' looking u'pon me.

18 They part my ' garments a'mong them : and cast ' lots up'on my ' vesture.

19 But be not thou far from ' me O ' Lord : thou art my succour ' haste ' thee to ' help me.

20 Deliver my soul ' from the ' sword : my darling ' from the ' power of the ' dog.

21 Save me from the ' lion's ' mouth : thou hast heard me also from a'mong the ' horns of the ' unicorns.

f 22 I will declare thy Name ' unto my ' brethren : in the midst of the congre'gation ' will I ' praise thee.

Change to Chant 65 overleaf

47

W. CROTCH

65

23 O praise the Lord ' ye that ' fear him : magnify him all ye of the
seed of Jacob, and fear him ' all ye ' seed of ' Israel;

24 For he hath not despised nor abhorred the low e'state of the ' poor :
he hath not hid his face from him, but when he called ' unto '
him he ' heard him.

25 My praise is of thee in the great ' congre'gation : my vows will I
perform in the ' sight of ' them that ' fear him.

26 The poor shall ' eat and be ' satisfied : they that seek after the Lord
shall praise him, your ' heart shall ' live for ' ever.

27 All the ends of the world shall remember themselves, and be turned '
unto the ' Lord : and all the kindreds of the ' nations shall '
worship be'fore him.

28 For the kingdom ' is the ' Lord's : and he is the ' Governor a-'
mong the ' people.

29 All such as be ' fat upon ' earth : have ' eaten ' and ' worshipped.

30 All they that go down into the dust shall ' kneel be'fore him : and
no man hath ' quickened his ' own ' soul.

31 My ' seed shall ' serve him : they shall be counted unto the '
Lord for a ' gene'ration.

32 They shall come, and the heavens shall de'clare his ' righteousness :
unto a people that shall be born ' whom the ' Lord hath ' made.

PSALM 23

J. TURLE

66

THE Lord ' is my ' shepherd : therefore ' can I ' lack ' nothing.

2 He shall feed me in a ' green ' pasture : and lead me forth be-'
side the ' waters of ' comfort.

48

3 He shall con'vert my ' soul : and bring me forth in the paths of righteousness ' for his ' Name's ' sake.

Cres 4 Yea though I walk through the valley of the shadow of death, I will ' fear no ' evil : for thou art with me, thy ' rod and thy ' staff ' comfort me.

5 Thou shalt prepare a table before me, against ' them that ' trouble me : thou hast anointed my head with oil ' and my ' cup shall be ' full.

f 6 But thy loving-kindness and mercy shall follow me, all the ' days of my ' life : and I will dwell in the ' house of the ' Lord for ' ever.

DAY 5   MORNING
PSALM 24

or

THE earth is the Lord's, and all that ' therein ' is : the compass of the world and ' they that ' dwell there'in.

2 For he hath founded it up'on the ' seas : and pre'pared it up'on the ' floods.

3 Who shall ascend into the ' hill of the ' Lord : or who shall rise up ' in his ' holy ' place?

4 Even he that hath clean hands and a ' pure ' heart : and that hath not lift up his mind unto vanity, nor ' sworn to de'ceive his ' neighbour.

5 He shall receive the blessing ' from the ' Lord : and righteousness from the ' God of ' his sal'vation.

6 This is the generation of ' them that ' seek him : even of them that ' seek thy ' face O ' Jacob.

49

or

68

Unison 7 Lift up your heads O ye gates, and be ye lift up ye ever'lasting '
doors : and the King of ' glory ' shall come ' in.

Men 8 Who is the ' King of ' glory : (*Unison*) it is the Lord strong and
mighty, even the ' Lord ' mighty in ' battle.

Unison 9 Lift up your heads O ye gates, and be ye lift up ye ever'lasting '
doors : and the King of ' glory ' shall come ' in.

Men 10 Who is the ' King of ' glory : (*Unison*) even the Lord of hosts, '
he is the ' King of ' glory.

PSALM 25

69

UNTO thee O Lord will I lift up my soul, my God I have put my '
trust in ' thee : O let me not be confounded, neither let mine '
enemies ' triumph ' over me.

2 For all they that hope in thee shall ' not be a'shamed : but such as
transgress without a cause ' shall be ' put to con'fusion.

3 Shew me thy ' ways O ' Lord : and ' teach me ' thy ' paths.

50

4 Lead me forth in thy ' truth and ' learn me : for thou art the God of my salvation, in thee hath been my ' hope ' all the day ' long.

5 Call to remembrance O Lord thy ' tender ' mercies : and thy loving-kindnesses, which ' have been ' ever of ' old.

6 O remember not the sins and offences ' of my ' youth : but according to thy mercy, think thou upon me O ' Lord ' for thy ' goodness.

7 Gracious and righteous ' is the ' Lord : therefore will he teach ' sinners ' in the ' way.

8 Them that are meek shall he ' guide in ' judgement : and such as are gentle ' them shall he ' learn his ' way.

9 All the paths of the Lord are ' mercy and ' truth : unto such as keep his ' covenant ' and his ' testimonies.

10 For thy Name's ' sake O ' Lord : be merciful unto my ' sin for ' it is ' great.

11 What man is he that ' feareth the ' Lord : him shall he teach in the ' way that ' he shall ' choose.

12 His soul shall ' dwell at ' ease : and his ' seed shall in'herit the ' land.

13 The secret of the Lord is among ' them that ' fear him : and ' he will ' shew them his ' covenant.

14 Mine eyes are ever looking ' unto the ' Lord : for he shall pluck my ' feet ' out of the ' net.

15 Turn thee unto me and have ' mercy up'on me : for I am ' desolate ' and in ' misery.

16 The sorrows of my heart ' are en'larged : O ' bring thou me ' out of my ' troubles.

17 Look upon my ad'versity and ' misery : and for'give me ' all my ' sin.

18 Consider mine enemies how ' many they ' are : and they bear a ' tyrannous ' hate a'gainst me.

19 O keep my ' soul and de'liver me : let me not be confounded, for I have ' put my ' trust in ' thee.

20 Let perfectness and righteous dealing ' wait up'on me : for my ' hope hath ' been in ' thee.

2nd Pt. 21 Deliver ' Israel O ' God : out of ' all ' his ' troubles.

PSALM 26

S. ELVEY

70

BE thou my Judge O Lord, for I have ' walk-ed ' innocently : my trust hath been also in the Lord ' therefore ' shall I not ' fall.

2 Examine me O ' Lord and ' prove me : try out my ' reins ' and my ' heart.

3 For thy loving-kindness is ever be'fore mine ' eyes : and I will ' walk in ' thy ' truth.

4 I have not dwelt with ' vain ' persons : neither will I have ' fellowship ' with the de'ceitful.

5 I have hated the congregation ' of the ' wicked : and will not ' sit a'mong the un'godly.

6 I will wash my hands in innocency ' O ' Lord : and ' so will I ' go to · thine ' altar;

7 That I may shew the ' voice of ' thanksgiving : and tell of ' all thy ' wondrous ' works.

8 Lord, I have loved the habitation ' of thy ' house : and the place ' where thine ' honour ' dwelleth.

9 O shut not up my soul ' with the ' sinners : nor my life ' with the ' blood'thirsty;

10 In whose ' hands is ' wickedness : and their right ' hand is ' full of ' gifts.

11 But as for me, I will ' walk ' innocently : O deliver me, and be ' merciful ' unto ' me.

12 My foot ' standeth ' right : I will praise the ' Lord in the ' congre'gations.

DAY 5 EVENING
PSALM 27

J. TURLE

71

THE Lord is my light and my salvation, whom then ' shall I ' fear : the Lord is the strength of my life, of whom then ' shall I ' be a'fraid?

2 When the wicked even mine enemies and my foes, came upon me to eat ' up my ' flesh : they ' stumbled ' and ' fell.

3 Though an host of men were laid against me, yet shall not my heart ' be a'fraid : and though there rose up war against me, yet will I ' put my ' trust in ' him.

4 One thing have I desired of the Lord which I ' will re'quire : even that I may dwell in the house of the Lord all the days of my life, to behold the fair beauty of the Lord ' and to ' visit his ' temple.

5 For in the time of trouble he shall hide me ' in his ' tabernacle : yea in the secret place of his dwelling shall he hide me, and set me up up'on a ' rock of ' stone.

6 And now shall he lift ' up mine ' head : above mine ' enemies ' round a'bout me.

7 Therefore will I offer in his dwelling an oblation with ' great ' gladness : I will sing and speak ' praises ' unto the ' Lord.

8 Hearken unto my voice O Lord, when I cry ' unto thee : have ' mercy up'on me and ' hear me.

9 My heart hath talked of thee, Seek ' ye my ' face : Thy face ' Lord ' will I ' seek.

10 O hide not thou thy ' face ' from me : nor cast thy ' servant a-' way in dis'pleasure.

11 Thou hast ' been my ' succour : leave me not neither forsake me O ' God of ' my sal'vation.

12 When my father and my ' mother for'sake me : the ' Lord ' taketh me ' up.

13 Teach me thy ' way O ' Lord : and lead me in the right ' way be'cause of mine ' enemies.

14 Deliver me not over into the ' will of mine ' adversaries : for there are false witnesses risen up against me, and ' such as ' speak ' wrong.

15 I should ' utterly have ' fainted : but that I believe verily to see the goodness of the ' Lord in the ' land of the ' living.

16 O tarry thou the ' Lord's ' leisure : be strong and he shall comfort thine heart, and ' put thou thy ' trust in the ' Lord.

PSALM 28

Unto thee will I cry O ' Lord my ' strength : think no scorn of me, lest if thou make as though thou hearest not, I become like them that go ' down ' into the ' pit.

2 Hear the voice of my humble petitions, when I cry ' unto ' thee : when I hold up my hands towards the mercy-seat ' of thy ' holy ' temple.

3 O pluck me not away, neither destroy me with the ungodly and ' wicked ' doers : which speak friendly to their neighbours, but imagine ' mischief ' in their ' hearts.

4 Reward them according ' to their ' deeds : and according to the wickedness ' of their ' own in'ventions.

5 Recompense them after the ' work of their ' hands : pay them ' that they ' have de'served.

6 For they regard not in their mind the works of the Lord, nor the operation ' of his ' hands : therefore shall he break them down ' and not ' build them ' up.

7 Praised ' be the ' Lord : for he hath heard the ' voice of my '
   humble pe'titions.

8 The Lord is my strength and my shield, my heart hath trusted in
   him and ' I am ' helped : therefore my heart danceth for joy, and
   in my ' song ' will I ' praise him.

9 The Lord ' is my ' strength : and he is the wholesome de'fence of '
   his A'nointed.

10 O save thy people, and give thy blessing unto ' thine in'heritance :
   feed them and ' set them ' up for ' ever.

PSALM 29

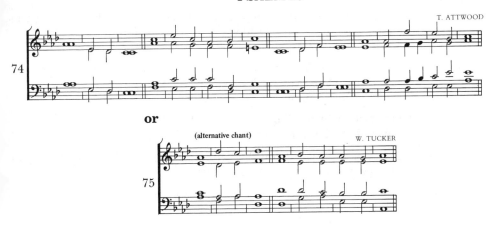

BRING unto the Lord O ye mighty, bring young rams ' unto the ' Lord :
   ascribe unto the ' Lord ' worship and ' strength.

2 Give the Lord the honour due ' unto his ' Name : worship the '
   Lord with ' holy ' worship.

or

3 It is the Lord that com'mandeth the ' waters : it is the glorious '
   God that ' maketh the ' thunder.

4 It is the Lord that ruleth the sea, the voice of the Lord is mighty in '
   oper'ation : the voice of the Lord ' is a ' glorious ' voice.

5 The voice of the Lord ' breaketh the ' cedar-trees : yea the Lord '
   breaketh the ' cedars of ' Libanus.

6 He maketh them also to skip ' like a ' calf : Libanus also and Sirion '
   like a ' young ' unicorn.

7 The voice of the Lord divideth the flames of fire, the voice of the
   Lord ' shaketh the ' wilderness : yea the Lord ' shaketh the '
   wilderness of ' Cades.

8 The voice of the Lord maketh the hinds to bring forth young, and
   discovereth the ' thick ' bushes : in his temple doth ' every man '
   speak of his ' honour.

9 The Lord sitteth a'bove the ' water-flood : and the Lord re-'
   maineth a ' King for ' ever.

10 The Lord shall give strength ' unto his ' people : the Lord shall give
   his ' people the ' blessing of ' peace.

DAY 6   MORNING

PSALM 30

I WILL magnify thee O Lord for thou hast ' set me ' up : and not made my ' foes to ' triumph ' over me.

2 O Lord my God I cried ' unto ' thee : and ' thou hast ' heal-ed ' me.

3 Thou Lord hast brought my soul ' out of ' hell: thou hast kept my life from ' them that go ' down to the ' pit.

4 Sing praises unto the Lord O ye ' saints of ' his : and give thanks unto him, for a re'membrance ' of his ' holiness.

5 For his wrath endureth but the twinkling of an eye, and in his ' pleasure is ' life : heaviness may endure for a night, but joy ' cometh ' in the ' morning.

6 And in my prosperity I said, I shall never ' be re'moved : thou Lord of thy goodness hast ' made my ' hill so ' strong.

7 Thou didst turn thy ' face ' from me : and ' I ' was ' troubled.

8 Then cried I unto ' thee O ' Lord : and gat me ' to my ' Lord right ' humbly.

9 What profit is there ' in my ' blood : when I go ' down ' to the ' pit?

10 Shall the dust give thanks ' unto ' thee : or ' shall it de'clare thy ' truth?

2nd Pt. 11 Hear O Lord and have ' mercy up'on me : Lord be ' thou ' my ' helper.

Change to Chant 76 overleaf

57

12 Thou hast turned my heaviness ' into ' joy : thou hast put off my sackcloth and ' girded ' me with ' gladness.

13 Therefore shall every good man sing of thy praise with'out ' ceasing : O my God, I will give thanks ' unto ' thee for ' ever.

PSALM 31

IN thee O Lord have I ' put my ' trust : let me never be put to confusion, de'liver me ' in thy ' righteousness.

2 Bow down thine ' ear to ' me : make ' haste · to de'liver ' me.

3 And be thou my strong rock and ' house of de'fence : that ' thou ' mayest ' save me.

4 For thou art my strong rock ' and my ' castle : be thou also my guide, and lead me ' for thy ' Name's ' sake.

5 Draw me out of the net that they have laid ' privily ' for me : for ' thou ' art my ' strength.

6 Into thy hands I com'mend my ' spirit : for thou hast redeemed me O ' Lord thou ' God of ' truth.

7 I have hated them that hold of super'stitious ' vanities : and my ' trust hath ' been in the ' Lord.

8 I will be glad and re'joice in thy ' mercy : for thou hast considered my trouble, and hast ' known my ' soul in ad'versities.

2nd   9 Thou hast not shut me up into the ' hand of the ' enemy : but hast
Part   set my ' feet in a ' large ' room.

58

10 Have mercy upon me O Lord for ' I am in ' trouble : and mine eye
    is consumed for very heaviness, yea my ' soul ' and my ' body.

11 For my life is waxen ' old with ' heaviness : and my ' years ' with '
    mourning.

12 My strength faileth me because of ' mine in'iquity : and my ' bones '
    are con'sumed.

13 I became a reproof among all mine enemies, but especially a-'
    mong my ' neighbours : and they of mine acquaintance were
    afraid of me, and they that did see me without con'veyed them-'
    selves ' from me.

14 I am clean forgotten, as a dead man ' out of ' mind : I am become '
    like a ' broken ' vessel.

15 For I have heard the blasphemy ' of the ' multitude : and fear is on
    every side, while they conspire together against me, and take
    their counsel to ' take a'way my ' life.

16 But my hope hath been in ' thee O ' Lord : I have said ' Thou art '
    my ' God.

17 My time is in thy hand, deliver me from the ' hand of mine '
    enemies : and from ' them that ' persecute ' me.

18 Shew thy servant the ' light of thy ' countenance : and save me '
    for thy ' mercy's ' sake.

19 Let me not be confounded O Lord, for I have ' called up'on thee : let
    the ungodly be put to confusion, and be put to ' silence ' in the '
    grave.

2nd   20 Let the lying lips be ' put to ' silence : which cruelly disdainfully
Part   and despitefully ' speak a'gainst the ' righteous.

Change to Chant 78 overleaf

78

21 O how plentiful is thy goodness, which thou hast laid up for ' them that ' fear thee : and that thou hast prepared for them that put their trust in thee, even be'fore the ' sons of ' men!

22 Thou shalt hide them privily by thine own presence, from the pro'voking of ' all men : thou shalt keep them secretly in thy tabernacle ' from the ' strife of ' tongues.

23 Thanks ' be to the ' Lord : for he hath shewed me marvellous great kindness ' in a ' strong ' city.

24 And when I made ' haste I ' said : I am cast out of the ' sight of ' thine ' eyes.

2nd 25 Nevertheless thou heardest the ' voice of my ' prayer : when I '
Part cried ' unto ' thee.

26 O love the Lord all ' ye his ' saints : for the Lord preserveth them that are faithful, and plenteously re'wardeth the ' proud ' doer.

27 Be strong and he shall e'stablish your ' heart : all ye that ' put your ' trust in the ' Lord.

<h3 style="text-align:center">DAY 6 EVENING
PSALM 32</h3>

80

BLESSED is he whose unrighteousness ' is for'given : and whose ' sin ' is ' covered.

2 Blessed is the man unto whom the Lord im'puteth no ' sin : and in whose ' spirit there ' is no ' guile.

3 For while I ' held my ' tongue : my bones consumed away ' through my ' daily com'plaining.

4 For thy hand is heavy upon me ' day and ' night : and my moisture is ' like the ' drought in ' summer.

5 I will acknowledge my sin ' unto ' thee : and mine un'righteousness ' have I not ' hid.

6 I said I will confess my sins ' unto the ' Lord : and so thou forgavest the ' wickedness ' of my ' sin.

7 For this shall every one that is godly make his prayer unto thee, in a time when thou ' mayest be ' found : but in the great water-floods ' they shall ' not come ' nigh him.

8 Thou art a place to hide me in, thou shalt pre'serve me from ' trouble : thou shalt compass me a'bout with ' songs of de-' liverance.

9 I will inform thee and teach thee in the way wherein ' thou shalt ' go : and I will ' guide thee ' with mine ' eye.

10 Be ye not like to horse and mule, which have no ' under'standing : whose mouths must be held with bit and bridle ' lest they ' fall up'on thee.

11 Great plagues remain ' for the un'godly : but whoso putteth his trust in the Lord, mercy embraceth ' him on ' every ' side.

12 Be glad O ye righteous, and rejoice ' in the ' Lord : and be joyful all ' ye that are ' true of ' heart.

PSALM 33

J. RANDALL

81

REJOICE in the Lord ' O ye ' righteous : for it becometh ' well the ' just to be ' thankful.

2 Praise the ' Lord with ' harp : sing praises unto him with the lute, and ' instrument ' of ten ' strings.

3 Sing unto the Lord a ' new ' song : sing praises lustily unto him ' with a ' good ' courage.

4 For the word of the ' Lord is ' true : and ' all his ' works are ' faithful.

5 He loveth ' righteousness and ' judgement : the earth is full of the ' goodness ' of the ' Lord.

6 By the word of the Lord were the ' heavens ' made : and all the hosts of them ' by the ' breath of his ' mouth.

61

J. RANDALL

81

7 He gathereth the waters of the sea together, as it were up'on an '
heap : and layeth up the deep as ' in a ' treasure'house.

8 Let all the earth ' fear the ' Lord : stand in awe of him, all ' ye that '
dwell in the ' world.

9 For he spake and ' it was ' done : he commanded ' and it ' stood '
fast.

10 The Lord bringeth the counsel of the ' heathen to ' nought : and
maketh the devices of the people to be of none effect, and casteth '
out the ' counsels of ' princes.

11 The counsel of the Lord shall en'dure for ' ever : and the thoughts
of his heart from gene'ration to ' gene'ration.

12 Blessed are the people whose God is the ' Lord Je'hovah : and
blessed are the folk, that he hath chosen to him to ' be '
his in'heritance.

13 The Lord looked down from heaven, and beheld all the ' children of '
men : from the habitation of his dwelling he considereth all '
them that ' dwell on the ' earth.

14 He fashioneth ' all the ' hearts of them : and under'standeth '
all their ' works.

15 There is no king that can be saved by the multitude ' of an ' host :
neither is any mighty man de'livered by ' much ' strength.

16 A horse is counted but a vain thing to ' save a ' man : neither shall
he deliver any man ' by his ' great ' strength.

17 Behold the eye of the Lord is upon ' them that ' fear him : and upon
them that ' put their ' trust in his ' mercy;

18 To deliver their ' soul from ' death : and to feed them ' in the '
time of ' dearth.

19 Our soul hath patiently tarried ' for the ' Lord : for he is our '
help and ' our ' shield.

20 For our heart shall re'joice in ' him : because we have hop-ed '
in his ' holy ' Name.

2nd 21 Let thy merciful kindness O Lord ' be up'on us : like as we do '
Part   put our ' trust in ' thee.

PSALM 34

F. A. G. OUSELEY

82

I WILL alway give thanks ' unto the ' Lord : his praise shall ' ever be ' in my ' mouth.

2 My soul shall make her ' boast in the ' Lord : the humble shall ' hear there'of and be ' glad.

3 O praise the ' Lord with ' me : and let us ' magnify his ' Name to-' gether.

4 I sought the Lord ' and he ' heard me : yea he delivered me ' out of ' all my ' fear.

5 They had an eye unto him ' and were ' lightened : and their ' faces were ' not a'shamed.

6 Lo the poor crieth and the Lord ' heareth ' him : yea and saveth him ' out of ' all his ' troubles.

* 7 The angel of the Lord tarrieth ' round about ' them that ' fear him : ' and de'livereth ' them.

8 O taste and see how ' gracious the ' Lord is : blessed is the ' man that ' trusteth in ' him.

9 O fear the Lord ye that ' are his ' saints : for they that ' fear him ' lack ' nothing.

10 The lions do lack and ' suffer ' hunger : but they who seek the Lord shall want no ' manner of ' thing that is ' good.

11 Come ye children, and hearken ' unto ' me : I will ' teach you the ' fear of the ' Lord.

12 What man is he that ' lusteth to ' live : and would ' fain see ' good ' days?

7 The angel of the Lord tarrieth round about ' them that ' fear him : and ' – de'livereth ' them.

F. A. G. OUSELEY

82

13 Keep thy ' tongue from ' evil : and thy lips ' that they ' speak no ' guile.

14 Eschew evil and ' do ' good : seek ' peace ' and en'sue it.

15 The eyes of the Lord are ' over the ' righteous : and his ears are ' open ' unto their ' prayers.

16 The countenance of the Lord is against ' them that do ' evil : to root out the remembrance ' of them ' from the ' earth.

17 The righteous cry and the ' Lord ' heareth them : and delivereth them ' out of ' all their ' troubles.

18 The Lord is nigh unto them that are of a ' contrite ' heart : and will save such as ' be of an ' humble ' spirit.

19 Great are the ' troubles of the ' righteous : but the Lord de-' livereth him ' out of ' all.

20 He keepeth ' all his ' bones : so that not ' one of ' them is ' broken.

21 But misfortune shall ' slay the un'godly : and they that hate the ' righteous ' shall be ' desolate.

22 The Lord delivereth the ' souls of his ' servants : and all they that put their trust in ' him shall ' not be ' destitute.

DAY 7   MORNING

PSALM 35

T. A. WALMISLEY

83

PLEAD thou my cause O Lord with ' them that ' strive with me : and fight thou against ' them that ' fight a'gainst me.

2 Lay hand upon the ' shield and ' buckler : and ' stand ' up to help me.

3 Bring forth the spear, and stop the way against ' them that persecute me : say unto my soul ' I am ' thy sal'vation.

4 Let them be confounded and put to shame, that seek ' after my '
soul : let them be turned back and brought to confusion, that
im'agine ' mischief ' for me.

5 Let them be as the dust be'fore the ' wind : and the angel of the '
Lord ' scattering ' them.

6 Let their way be ' dark and ' slippery : and let the angel of the '
Lord ' persecute ' them.

7 For they have privily laid their net to destroy me with'out a ' cause :
yea, even without a cause have they ' made a ' pit for my ' soul.

8 Let a sudden destruction come upon him unawares, and his net that
he hath laid privily ' catch him'self : that he may fall ' into his '
own ' mischief.

9 And my soul be joyful ' in the ' Lord : it shall re'joice in '
his sal'vation.

10 All my bones shall say, Lord who is like unto thee, who deliverest
the poor from him that ' is too ' strong for him : yea the poor, and
him that is in ' misery from ' him that ' spoileth him?

11 False witnesses did ' rise ' up : they laid to my charge ' things that '
I ' knew not.

12 They rewarded me ' evil for ' good : to the great dis'comfort ' of my '
soul.

13 Nevertheless when they were sick I put on sackcloth, and humbled
my ' soul with ' fasting : and my prayer shall turn ' into mine '
own ' bosom.

14 I behaved myself as though it had been my friend ' or my '
brother : I went heavily, as one that ' mourneth ' for his '
mother.

15 But in mine adversity they rejoiced, and gathered them-'
selves to'gether : yea the very abjects came together
against me unawares, making ' mouths at ' me and ' ceased not.

16 With the flatterers were ' busy ' mockers : who gnashed up'on me '
with their ' teeth.

17 Lord how long wilt thou ' look upon ' this : O deliver my soul from
the calamities which they bring on me, and my ' darling '
from the ' lions.

18 So will I give thee thanks in the great ' congre'gation : I will '
praise thee a'mong much ' people.

T. A. WALMISLEY

83

19 O let not them that are mine enemies triumph over ' me un'godly :
neither let them wink with their eyes that ' hate me with'out a '
cause.

20 And why? their communing is ' not for ' peace : but they imagine
deceitful words against them that are ' quiet ' in the ' land.

21 They gaped upon me with their ' mouths and ' said : Fie on thee, fie
on thee, we ' saw it ' with our ' eyes.

22 This thou hast ' seen O ' Lord : hold not thy tongue then, go not '
far from ' me O ' Lord.

23 Awake and stand up to ' judge my ' quarrel : avenge thou my
cause my ' God and ' my ' Lord.

24 Judge me O Lord my God according ' to thy ' righteousness : and '
let them not ' triumph ' over me.

25 Let them not say in their hearts, There, there, ' so would we '
have it : neither let them say, ' We ' have de'voured him.

26 Let them be put to confusion and shame together that rejoice '
at my ' trouble : let them be clothed with rebuke and dishonour
that ' boast them'selves a'gainst me.

27 Let them be glad and rejoice that favour my ' righteous ' dealing :
yea let them say alway, Blessed be the Lord who hath pleasure
in the pros'perity ' of his ' servant.

28 And as for my tongue it shall be talking ' of thy ' righteousness :
and of thy ' praise ' all the day ' long.

PSALM 36

Vss 1-4

J. HARRISON

84

MY heart sheweth me the wickedness ' of the un'godly : that there is
no fear of ' God be'fore his ' eyes.

2 For he flattereth himself in his ' own ' sight : until his abominable '
  sin be ' found ' out.

3 The words of his mouth are unrighteous and ' full of de'ceit : he
  hath left off to behave himself wisely ' and to ' do ' good.

4 He imagineth mischief upon his bed, and hath set himself in '
  no good ' way : neither doth he abhor ' any thing ' that is ' evil.

85

5 Thy mercy O Lord reacheth ' unto the ' heavens : and thy '
  faithfulness ' unto the ' clouds.

6 Thy righteousness standeth like the ' strong ' mountains : thy
  judgements are ' like the ' great ' deep.

7 Thou Lord shalt save both man and beast, How excellent is thy '
  mercy O ' God : and the children of men shall put their trust
  under the ' shadow ' of thy ' wings.

8 They shall be satisfied with the plenteousness ' of thy ' house :
  and thou shalt give them drink of thy ' pleasures as ' out of the '
  river.

9 For with thee is the ' well of ' life : and in thy ' light shall ' we see '
  light.

10 O continue forth thy loving-kindness unto ' them that ' know thee :
   and thy righteousness unto ' them that are ' true of ' heart.

11 O let not the foot of pride ' come a'gainst me : and let not the
   hand of the un'godly ' cast me ' down.

12 There are they fallen ' all that work ' wickedness : they are cast
   down and shall ' not be ' able to ' stand.

DAY 7 EVENING
PSALM 37

86

FRET not thyself be'cause of · the un'godly : neither be thou envious
a'gainst the ' evil'doers.

2 For they shall soon be cut ' down like the ' grass : and be withered '
even · as the ' green ' herb.

3 Put thou thy trust in the Lord and be ' doing ' good : dwell in the
land, and ' verily ' thou shalt be ' fed.

4 Delight thou ' in the ' Lord : and he shall ' give thee thy '
heart's de'sire.

5 Commit thy way unto the Lord, and put thy ' trust in ' him : and '
he shall ' bring it to ' pass.

6 He shall make thy righteousness as ' clear as the ' light : and thy
just ' dealing ' as the ' noon-day.

7 Hold thee still in the Lord, and abide ' patiently up'on him : but
grieve not thyself at him whose way doth prosper, against the
man that doeth ' after ' evil ' counsels.

8 Leave off from wrath and let ' go dis'pleasure : fret not thyself, else
shalt thou be ' moved to ' do ' evil.

9 Wicked doers shall be ' rooted ' out : and they that patiently abide
the Lord ' those shall in'herit the ' land.

10 Yet a little while, and the ungodly shall be ' clean ' gone : thou
shalt look after his place and ' he shall ' be a'way.

11 But the meek-spirited shall pos'sess the ' earth : and shall be
re'freshed in the ' multitude of ' peace.

12 The ungodly seeketh counsel a'gainst the ' just : and gnasheth
up'on him ' with his ' teeth.

13 The Lord shall ' laugh him to ' scorn : for he hath ' seen that his
day is ' coming.

14 The ungodly have drawn out the sword and have ' bent their ' bow
to cast down the poor and needy, and to slay such as are of a
right ' conver'sation.

15 Their sword shall go through their ' own ' heart : and their ' bow '
shall be ' broken.

16 A small thing that the ' righteous ' hath : is better than great '
riches ' of the un'godly.

17 For the arms of the ungodly ' shall be ' broken : and the '
Lord up'holdeth the ' righteous.

18 The Lord knoweth the ' days of the ' godly : and their inheritance '
shall en'dure for'ever.

19 They shall not be confounded in the ' perilous ' time : and in the
days of dearth ' they shall ' have e'nough.

20 As for the ungodly they shall perish, and the enemies of the Lord
shall consume as the ' fat of ' lambs : yea even as the smoke shall '
they con'sume a'way.

21 The ungodly borroweth and payeth ' not a'gain : but the '
righteous is ' merciful and ' liberal.

22 Such as are blessed of God shall pos'sess the ' land : and they that
are cursed of him ' shall be ' rooted ' out.

87

23 The Lord ordereth a ' good man's ' going : and maketh his way
ac'ceptable ' to him'self.

24 Though he fall he shall not be ' cast a'way : for the Lord up-'
holdeth him ' with his ' hand.

25 I have been young and ' now am ' old : and yet saw I never the
righteous forsaken, nor his ' seed ' begging their ' bread.

26 The righteous is ever ' merciful and ' lendeth : and ' his ' seed is '
blessed.

27 Flee from evil, and do the ' thing that is ' good : and ' dwell for '
ever'more.

28 For the Lord loveth the ' thing that is ' right : he forsaketh not his
that be godly, but ' they are pre'served for ' ever.

29 The unrighteous ' shall be ' punished : as for the seed of the ungodly '
it shall be ' rooted ' out.

30 The righteous shall in'herit the ' land : and ' dwell there'in for '
ever.

Vss 23-end

SKARRATT

87

31 The mouth of the righteous is ' exercised in ' wisdom : and his '
tongue will be ' talking of ' judgement.

32 The law of his God is ' in his ' heart : and his ' goings ' shall not '
slide.

33 The ungodly ' seeth the ' righteous : and ' seeketh oc'casion to '
slay him.

34 The Lord will not leave him ' in his ' hand : nor con'demn him '
when he is ' judged.

35 Hope thou in the Lord and keep his way, and he shall promote thee
that thou shalt pos'sess the ' land : when the ungodly shall '
perish ' thou shalt ' see it.

36 I myself have seen the ungodly in ' great ' power : and flourishing '
like a ' green ' bay-tree.

2nd Part

37 I went by, and ' lo he was ' gone : I sought him, but his ' place could '
no where be ' found.

38 Keep innocency, and take heed unto the ' thing that is ' right : for
that shall ' bring a man ' peace at the ' last.

39 As for the transgressors they shall ' perish to'gether : and the end
of the ungodly is, they shall be ' rooted ' out at the ' last.

40 But the salvation of the righteous ' cometh of the ' Lord : who is
also their ' strength in the ' time of ' trouble.

41 And the Lord shall stand by ' them and ' save them : he shall
deliver them from the ungodly and shall save them, because they '
put their ' trust in ' him.

DAY 8   MORNING

PSALM 38

J. TURLE

88

Put me not to rebuke O Lord ' in thine ' anger : neither chasten me ' in thy ' heavy dis'pleasure.

2 For thine arrows stick ' fast in ' me : and thy ' hand ' presseth me ' sore.

3 There is no health in my flesh because of ' thy dis'pleasure : neither is there any rest in my bones by ' reason ' of my ' sin.

4 For my wickednesses are gone ' over my ' head : and are like a sore burden too ' heavy for ' me to ' bear.

*   5 My ' wounds ' stink and ' are cor'rupt : through ' my ' foolishness.

6 I am brought into so great ' trouble and ' misery : that I go ' mourning ' all the day ' long.

7 For my loins are filled with a ' sore dis'ease : and there is no ' whole part ' in my ' body.

8 I am feeble and ' sore ' smitten : I have roared for the very dis'quietness ' of my ' heart.

9 Lord thou knowest all ' my de'sire : and my groaning ' is not ' hid from ' thee.

10 My heart panteth my ' strength hath ' failed me : and the ' sight of mine ' eyes is ' gone from me.

11 My lovers and my neighbours did stand looking up'on my ' trouble : and my kinsmen ' stood a'far ' off.

12 They also that sought after my ' life laid ' snares for me : and they that went about to do me evil talked of wickedness, and imagined deceit ' all the ' day ' long.

13 As for me, I was like a deaf ' man and ' heard not : and as one that is dumb who ' doth not ' open his ' mouth.

14 I became even as a man that ' heareth ' not : and in whose ' mouth are ' no re'proofs.

My wounds stink and are cor - rupt: through my foolishness.

5 My wounds stink and ' are cor'rupt : through ' my ' foolish'ness.

J. TURLE

88

15 For in thee O Lord have I ' put my ' trust : thou shalt answer for '
me O ' Lord my ' God.

16 I have required that they even mine enemies, should not ' triumph '
over me : for when my foot slipped, they re'joic-ed ' greatly a-'
gainst me.

17 And I truly am ' set in the ' plague : and my heaviness is ' ever '
in my ' sight.

18 For I will con'fess my ' wickedness : and be ' sorry ' for my ' sin.

19 But mine enemies live ' and are ' mighty : and they that hate me '
wrongfully are ' many in ' number.

20 They also that reward evil for good ' are a'gainst me : because I
follow the ' thing that ' good ' is.

21 Forsake me not O ' Lord my ' God : be not ' thou ' far ' from me.

22 Haste ' thee to ' help me : O Lord ' God of ' my sal'vation.

PSALM 39

J. L. ROGERS

89

I SAID I will take heed ' to my ' ways : that I of'fend not ' in my '
tongue.

2 I will keep my mouth as it ' were with a ' bridle : while the un-'
godly is ' in my ' sight.

3 I held my tongue and ' spake ' nothing : I kept silence, yea even
from good words, but it was ' pain and ' grief to ' me.

4 My heart was hot within me, and while I was thus musing the ' fire '
kindled : and at the ' last I ' spake with my ' tongue;

5 Lord let me know mine end and the ' number · of my ' days : that
I may be certified how ' long I ' have to ' live.

6 Behold thou hast made my days as it were a ' span ' long : and mine
   age is even as nothing in respect of thee, and verily every man
   living is ' alto'gether ' vanity.

7 For man walketh in a vain shadow, and disquieteth him'self in '
   vain : he heapeth up riches, and ' cannot tell ' who shall '
   gather them.

8 And now Lord ' what is my ' hope : truly my ' hope is ' even in '
   thee.

9 Deliver me from all ' mine of'fences : and make me not a re'buke '
   unto the ' foolish.

10 I became dumb, and opened ' not my ' mouth : for ' it was ' thy '
   doing.

11 Take thy plague a'way ' from me : I am even consumed by the '
   means of thy ' heavy ' hand.

12 When thou with rebukes dost chasten man for sin, thou makest his
   beauty to consume away, like as it were a moth ' fretting a '
   garment : every man ' therefore ' is but ' vanity.

13 Hear my prayer O Lord, and with thine ears con'sider my ' calling :
   hold not thy ' peace ' at my ' tears.

14 For I am a ' stranger with ' thee : and a sojourner as ' all my '
   fathers ' were.

2nd 15 O spare me a little that I may re'cover my ' strength : before I go '
Part   hence and be ' no more ' seen.

PSALM 40

W. MARSH

90

I WAITED patiently ' for the ' Lord : and he inclined unto ' me and '
   heard my ' calling.

2 He brought me also out of the horrible pit, out of the ' mire and '
   clay : and set my feet upon the rock, and ' ordered ' my ' goings.

3 And he hath put a new ' song in my ' mouth : even a '
   thanks · giving ' unto our ' God.

4 Many shall ' see it and ' fear : and shall ' put their ' trust in the '
   Lord.

5 Blessed is the man that hath set his ' hope in the ' Lord : and turned not unto the proud, and to such as ' go a'bout with ' lies.

6 O Lord my God, great are the wondrous works which thou hast done, like as be also thy thoughts which ' are to ' us-ward : and yet there is no man that ' ordereth them ' unto ' thee.

7 If I should de'clare them and ' speak of them : they should be more than I am ' able ' to ex'press.

8 Sacrifice and meat-offering thou ' wouldest ' not : but mine ' ears hast ' thou ' opened.

9 Burnt-offerings and sacrifice for sin hast thou ' not re'quired : then ' said I ' Lo I ' come,

10 In the volume of the book it is written of me, that I should fulfil thy will ' O my ' God : I am content to do it, yea thy law ' is with-'in my ' heart.

11 I have declared thy righteousness in the great ' congre'gation : lo I will not refrain my lips O ' Lord and ' that thou ' knowest.

12 I have not hid thy righteousness with'in my ' heart : my talk hath been of thy ' truth and of ' thy sal'vation.

2nd Part 13 I have not kept back thy loving ' mercy and ' truth : from the ' great ' congre'gation.

14 Withdraw not thou thy mercy from ' me O ' Lord : let thy loving-kindness and thy ' truth ' alway pre'serve me.

15 For innumerable troubles are come about me, my sins have taken such hold upon me, that I am not able to ' look ' up : yea they are more in number than the hairs of my head, and my ' heart hath ' fail-ed ' me.

16 O Lord let it be thy ' pleasure · to de'liver me : make ' haste O ' Lord to ' help me.

17 Let them be ashamed and confounded together, that seek after my soul ' to de'stroy it : let them be driven backward and put to re'buke that ' wish me ' evil.

18 Let them be desolate and re'warded with ' shame : that say unto me, Fie up'on thee ' fie up'on thee.

19 Let all those that seek thee be joyful and ' glad in ' thee : and let such as love thy salvation say ' alway The ' Lord be ' praised.

20 As for me I am ' poor and ' needy : but the ' Lord ' careth ' for me.

21 Thou art my helper ' and re'deemer : make no long ' tarrying ' O my ' God.

DAY 8   EVENING

PSALM 41

91

BLESSED is he that considereth the ' poor and ' needy : the Lord shall deliver him ' in the ' time of ' trouble.

2 The Lord preserve him and keep him alive, that he may be blessed up'on ' earth : and deliver not thou him ' into the ' will of his ' enemies.

3 The Lord comfort him when he lieth sick up'on his ' bed : make thou all his ' bed ' in his ' sickness.

4 I said Lord be merciful ' unto ' me : heal my soul for ' I have ' sinned a'gainst thee.

5 Mine enemies speak ' evil ' of me : When shall he die ' and his ' name ' perish?

6 And if he come to see me he ' speaketh ' vanity : and his heart conceiveth falsehood within himself, and when he ' cometh ' forth he ' telleth it.

7 All mine enemies whisper to'gether a'gainst me : even against me do ' they im'agine this ' evil.

8 Let the sentence of guiltiness pro'ceed a'gainst him : and now that he lieth ' let him rise ' up no ' more.

9 Yea even mine own familiar friend ' whom I ' trusted : who did also eat of my bread hath ' laid great ' wait for ' me.

10 But be thou merciful unto ' me O ' Lord : raise thou me up again ' and I ' shall re'ward them.

11 By this I know thou ' favourest ' me : that mine enemy ' doth not ' triumph a'gainst me.

12 And when I am in my health ' thou up'holdest me : and shalt set me be'fore thy ' face for ' ever.

2nd Pt. 13 Blessed be the Lord ' God of ' Israel : world without ' end. ' A'men.
Unison

PSALM 42

LIKE as the hart de'sireth the ' water-brooks : so longeth my soul ' after ' thee O ' God.

2 My soul is athirst for God, yea even for the ' living ' God : when shall I come to appear be'fore the ' presence of ' God?

3 My tears have been my meat ' day and ' night : while they daily say unto me, Where is ' now ' thy ' God?

4 Now when I think thereupon, I pour out my heart ' by my'self : for I went with the multitude, and brought them forth ' into the ' house of ' God;

2nd   5 In the voice of ' praise and ' thanksgiving : among such as ' keep '
Part   holy ' day.

p   6 Why art thou so full of heaviness ' O my ' soul : and why art thou ' so dis'quiet·ed with'in me?

f   7 Put thy ' trust in ' God : for I will yet give him ' thanks for the ' help of his ' countenance.

8 My God my soul is ' vexed with'in me : therefore will I remember thee concerning the land of Jordan, and the ' little ' hill of ' Hermon.

9 One deep calleth another, because of the ' noise of the ' water pipes : all thy ' waves and ' storms are gone ' over me.

10 The Lord hath granted his loving-kindness ' in the ' day-time : and in the night-season did I sing of him, and made my prayer ' unto the ' God of my ' life.

11 I will say unto the God of my strength, Why hast ' thou for-' gotten me : why go I thus heavily, while the ' enemy op'presseth ' me?

12 My bones are smitten asunder ' as with a ' sword : while mine enemies that trouble me ' cast me ' in the ' teeth;

13 Namely while they say ' daily ' unto me : Where is ' now ' thy ' God?

p   14 Why art thou so vexed ' O my ' soul : and why art thou ' so dis'quiet·ed with'in me?

f   15 O put thy ' trust in ' God : for I will yet thank him, which is the help of my ' countenance ' and my ' God.

PSALM 43   (Chant 92)

GIVE sentence with me O God, and defend my cause against the un'godly ' people : O deliver me from the de'ceitful and ' wicked ' man.

2 For thou art the God of my strength, why hast thou ' put me ' from thee : and why go I so heavily, while the ' enemy op-' presseth ' me?

77

92

93

3 O send out thy light and thy truth that ' they may ' lead me : and bring me unto thy holy ' hill and ' to thy ' dwelling.

4 And that I may go unto the altar of God, even unto the God of my ' joy and ' gladness : and upon the harp will I give thanks unto ' thee O ' God my ' God.

p   5 Why art thou so heavy ' O my ' soul : and why art thou ' so dis'quiet·ed with'in me?

f   6 O put thy ' trust in ' God : for I will yet give him thanks, which is the help of my ' countenance ' and my ' God.

DAY 9   MORNING

PSALM 44

94

We have heard with our ears O God our ' fathers have ' told us : what thou hast done ' in their ' time of ' old;

2 How thou hast driven out the heathen with thy hand, and planted them ' in : how thou hast destroyed the ' nations and cast them ' out.

3 For they gat not the land in possession through their ' own ' sword :
   neither was it their own ' arm that ' help-ed ' them;

4 But thy right hand and thine arm and the ' light of thy '
   countenance : because thou hadst a ' favour ' unto ' them.

5 Thou art my ' King O ' God : send ' help ' unto ' Jacob.

6 Through thee will we over'throw our ' enemies : and in thy Name
   will we tread them under that ' rise ' up a'gainst us.

7 For I will not trust ' in my ' bow : it is not my ' sword ' that shall '
   help me;

8 But it is thou that savest us ' from our ' enemies : and puttest '
   them · to con'fusion that ' hate us.

2nd   9 We make our boast of God ' all day ' long : and will ' praise thy '
Part   Name for ' ever.

10 But now thou art far off, and puttest ' us · to con'fusion : and '
   goest not ' forth with our ' armies.

11 Thou makest us to turn our backs up'on our ' enemies : so that they
   which ' hate us ' spoil our ' goods.

12 Thou lettest us be eaten ' up like ' sheep : and hast ' scattered us a-'
   mong the ' heathen.

13 Thou sellest thy ' people for ' nought : and ' takest no ' money '
   for them.

14 Thou makest us to be re'buked of our ' neighbours : to be laughed
   to scorn, and had in derision of ' them that are ' round a'bout us.

15 Thou makest us to be a by-word a'mong the ' heathen : and that
   the ' people ' shake their ' heads at us.

16 My confusion is ' daily be'fore me : and the ' shame of my '
   face hath ' covered me;

17 For the voice of the slanderer ' and blas'phemer : for the ' enemy '
   and a'venger.

18 And though all this be come upon us, yet do we ' not for'get thee :
   nor behave ourselves ' frowardly ' in thy ' covenant.

19 Our heart is not ' turn-ed ' back : neither our ' steps gone '
   out of thy ' way;   *Vs. 20 Overleaf 2nd part*

94

DIBDIN

2nd 20 No not when thou hast smitten us into the ' place of ' dragons : and
Part   covered us ' with the ' shadow of ' death.

21 If we have forgotten the Name of our God, and holden up our hands
to any ' strange ' god : shall not God search it out? for he knoweth
the very ' secrcts ' of the ' heart.

22 For thy sake also are we killed ' all the day ' long : and are counted
as sheep ap'pointed ' to be ' slain.

23 Up Lord, why ' sleepest ' thou : awake, and be not ' absent from '
us for ' ever.

24 Wherefore hidest ' thou thy ' face : and for'gettest our ' misery and '
trouble?

25 For our soul is brought low, even ' unto the ' dust : our belly '
cleaveth ' unto the ' ground.

26 Arise and ' help ' us : and deliver us ' for thy ' mercy's ' sake.

PSALM 45

95

My tongue is the pen: of a read - y writer.

Single Chant.

My heart is inditing of a ' good ' matter : I speak of the things which
I have ' made ' unto the ' King.

½   2 My tongue is the ' pen : of a ' ready ' writer.

2 My tongue ' is the ' pen : of ' – a ' ready ' writer.

3 Thou art fairer than the ' children of ' men : full of grace are thy
   lips, because God hath ' bless-ed ' thee for ' ever.

4 Gird thee with thy sword upon thy thigh O ' thou most ' Mighty :
   according to thy ' worship ' and re'nown.

5 Good luck have thou ' with thine ' honour : ride on because of the
   word of truth, of meekness and righteousness, and thy right hand
   shall ' teach thee ' terrible ' things.

6 Thy arrows are very sharp, and the people shall be subdued ' unto '
   thee : even in the midst a'mong the ' King's ' enemies.

7 Thy seat O God en'dureth for ' ever : the sceptre of thy kingdom '
   is a ' right ' sceptre.

8 Thou hast loved righteousness and ' hated in'iquity : wherefore God
   even thy God, hath anointed thee with the oil of ' gladness a-'
   bove thy ' fellows.

9 All thy garments smell of myrrh ' aloes and ' cassia : out of the
   ivory palaces whereby ' they have ' made thee ' glad.

10 Kings' daughters were among thy ' honour · able ' women : upon
   thy right hand did stand the queen in a vesture of gold, wrought
   a'bout with ' divers ' colours.

96

11 Hearken O daughter and consider, in'cline thine ' ear : forget also
   thine own people ' and thy ' father's ' house.

12 So shall the King have pleasure ' in thy ' beauty : for he is thy Lord '
   God and ' worship thou ' him.

13 And the daughter of Tyre shall be ' there with a ' gift : like as the
   rich also among the people shall make their ' suppli'cation be-'
   fore thee.

14 The King's daughter is all ' glorious with'in : her clothing ' is of '
   wrought ' gold.

15 She shall be brought unto the King in ' raiment of ' needle-work :
   the virgins that be her fellows shall bear her company, and shall
   be ' brought ' unto ' thee.

16 With joy and gladness shall ' they be ' brought : and shall enter '
   into the ' King's ' palace.   *Change to Chant 95 overleaf*

95

17 Instead of thy fathers thou ' shalt have ' children : whom thou mayest make ' princes in ' all ' lands.

18 I will remember thy Name from one generation ' to an'other : therefore shall the people give thanks unto thee ' world with'out ' end.

PSALM 46

97

GOD is our ' hope and ' strength : a very ' present ' help in ' trouble.

2 Therefore will we not fear, though the ' earth be ' moved : and though the hills be carried ' into the ' midst of the ' sea ;

3 Though the waters thereof ' rage and ' swell : and though the mountains shake at the ' tempest ' of the ' same.

4 The rivers of the flood thereof shall make glad the ' city of ' God : the holy place of the tabernacle ' of the ' most ' Highest.

5 God is in the midst of her, therefore shall she ' not be re'moved : God shall ' help her and ' that right ' early.

6 The heathen make much ado and the ' kingdoms are ' moved : but God hath shewed his voice, and the ' earth shall ' melt a'way.

2nd Pt.
Unison 7 The Lord of ' hosts is ' with us : the God of ' Jacob ' is our ' refuge.

8 O come hither and behold the ' works of the ' Lord : what destruction he hath ' brought up'on the ' earth.

9 He maketh wars to cease in ' all the ' world : he breaketh the bow, and knappeth the spear in sunder, and burneth the ' chariots ' in the ' fire.

10 Be still then and know that ' I am ' God : I will be exalted among the heathen, and I will be ex'alted ' in the ' earth.

Unison 11 The Lord of ' hosts is ' with us : the God of ' Jacob ' is our ' refuge.

DAY 9 EVENING

PSALM 47

T. S. DUPUIS

98

O CLAP your hands together ' all ye ' people : O sing unto ' God with the ' voice of ' melody.

2 For the Lord is high and ' to be ' feared : he is the great ' King upon ' all the ' earth.

3 He shall subdue the ' people ' under us : and the ' nations ' under our ' feet.

4 He shall choose out an ' heritage ' for us : even the worship of ' Jacob ' whom he ' loved.

2nd 5 God is gone up with a ' merry ' noise : and the ' Lord with the ' *Part* sound of the ' trump.

6 O sing praises sing praises ' unto our ' God : O sing praises sing ' praises ' unto our ' King.

7 For God is the King of ' all the ' earth : sing ye ' praises with ' under'standing.

8 God reigneth ' over the ' heathen : God sitteth up'on his ' holy ' seat.

9 The princes of the people are joined unto the people of the ' God of ' Abraham : for God which is very high exalted, doth defend the ' earth as it ' were with a ' shield.

PSALM 48

J. ROBINSON

99

GREAT is the Lord and ' highly · to be ' praised : in the city of our God,
  even up'on his ' holy ' hill.

2 The hill of Sion is a fair place, and the joy of the ' whole ' earth :
  upon the north-side lieth the city of the great King, God is well
  known in her palaces ' as a ' sure ' refuge.

3 For lo the ' kings of the ' earth : are gathered and ' gone '
  by to'gether.

4 They marvelled to ' see such ' things : they were astonished and '
  suddenly ' cast ' down.

5 Fear came there upon ' them and ' sorrow : as upon a ' woman '
  in her ' travail.

*   6 Thou shalt ' break the ' ships of the ' sea : ' through the ' east '
  wind.

2nd   7 Like as we have heard, so have we seen in the city of the Lord of
Part   hosts, in the city of ' our ' God : God up'holdeth the ' same for'
  ever.

8 We wait for thy loving'kindness O ' God : in the ' midst of ' thy '
  temple.

9 O God according to thy Name, so is thy praise unto the ' world's '
  end : thy right ' hand is ' full of ' righteousness.

10 Let the mount Sion rejoice, and the daughter of ' Judah be ' glad :
  be'cause of ' thy ' judgements.

6 Thou shalt break the ' ships of the ' sea : through ' – the ' east ' wind.

11 Walk about Sion and go ' round a'bout her : and ' tell the ' towers there'of.

12 Mark well her bulwarks, set ' up her ' houses : that ye may tell ' them that ' come ' after.

13 For this God is our God for ' ever and ' ever : he shall be our ' guide ' unto ' death.

PSALM 49

O HEAR ye this ' all ye ' people : ponder it with your ears, all ' ye that ' dwell in the ' world;

* 2 High and ' low ' rich and ' poor : ' one ' with an'other.

3 My mouth shall ' speak of ' wisdom : and my heart shall ' muse of ' under'standing.

4 I will incline mine ' ear to the ' parable : and shew my dark ' speech up'on the ' harp.

5 Wherefore should I fear in the ' days of ' wickedness : and when the wickedness of my heels ' compasseth me ' round a'bout?

6 There be some that put their ' trust in their ' goods : and boast themselves in the ' multitude ' of their ' riches.

7 But no man may de'liver his ' brother : nor make agreement ' unto ' God ' for him;

8 For it cost more to re'deem their ' souls : so that he must let ' that a'lone for ' ever;

2 High and low ' rich and ' poor : one ' — ' with an'other.

"Cambridge Chant"

100

9 Yea though he ' live ' long : and ' see ' not the ' grave.

10 For he seeth that wise men also die and ' perish to'gether : as well as the ignorant and foolish and ' leave their ' riches for ' other.

11 And yet they think that their houses shall con'tinue for ' ever : and that their dwelling-places shall endure from one generation to another, and call the lands ' after their ' own ' names.

12 Nevertheless man will not a'bide in ' honour : seeing he may be compared unto the beasts that perish, ' this is the ' way of ' them.

13 This ' is their ' foolishness : and their pos'terity ' praise their ' saying.

14 They lie in the hell like sheep, death gnaweth upon them, and the righteous shall have domination over them ' in the ' morning : their beauty shall consume in the ' sepulchre ' out of their ' dwelling.

15 But God hath delivered my soul from the ' place of ' hell : for ' he ' shall re'ceive me.

16 Be not thou afraid though ' one be made ' rich : or if the ' glory · of his ' house · be in'creased;

17 For he shall carry nothing away with him ' when he ' dieth : neither ' shall his ' pomp ' follow him.

18 For while he lived he counted himself an ' happy ' man : and so long as thou doest well unto thyself, ' men will · speak ' good of ' thee.

19 He shall follow the generation ' of his ' fathers : and shall ' never ' see ' light.

20 Man being in honour hath no ' under'standing : but is compared ' unto the ' beasts that ' perish.

DAY 10   MORNING
PSALM 50

P. HENLEY

101

THE Lord even the most mighty ' God hath ' spoken : and called the world, from the rising up of the sun unto the ' going ' down there'of.

*   2 Out ' of ' Sion ' hath God ap'peared : in ' perfect ' beauty.

3 Our God shall come and shall ' not keep ' silence : there shall go before him a consuming fire, and a mighty tempest shall be ' stirred up ' round a'bout him.

4 He shall call the heaven ' from a'bove : and the earth that ' he may ' judge his ' people.

5 Gather my saints together ' unto ' me : those that have made a ' covenant with ' me with ' sacrifice.

6 And the heavens shall de'clare his ' righteousness : for ' God is ' Judge him'self.

7 Hear O my people and ' I will ' speak : I myself will testify against thee O Israel, for I am God ' even ' thy ' God.

8 I will not reprove thee because of thy sacrifices, or for thy ' burnt-' offerings : because they ' were not ' alway be'fore me.

9 I will take no bullock ' out of thine ' house : nor ' he-goat ' out of thy ' folds.

10 For all the beasts of the ' forest are ' mine : and so are the cattle up'on a ' thousand ' hills.

11 I know all the fowls up'on the ' mountains : and the wild beasts of the ' field are ' in my ' sight.

12 If I be hungry I ' will not ' tell thee : for the whole world is mine and ' all that ' is there'in.

13 Thinkest thou that I will ' eat bulls' ' flesh : and ' drink the ' blood of ' goats?

14 Offer unto ' God ' thanksgiving : and pay thy vows ' unto the ' most ' Highest.

2nd   15 And call upon me in the ' time of ' trouble : so will I ' hear thee and '
Part   thou shalt ' praise me.

2 Out of Sion hath ' God ap'peared : in ' per'fect ' beauty.

P. HENLEY

101

16 But unto the un'godly said ' God : Why dost thou preach my laws,
and takest my ' covenant ' in thy ' mouth;

17 Whereas thou hatest to ' be re'formed : and hast ' cast my '
words be'hind thee?

18 When thou sawest a thief thou consentedst ' unto ' him : and hast
been par'taker ' with the a'dulterers.

19 Thou hast let thy ' mouth speak ' wickedness : and with thy tongue '
thou hast set ' forth de'ceit.

20 Thou satest and spakest a'gainst thy ' brother : yea and hast
slandered thine ' own ' mother's ' son.

21 These things hast thou done and I held my tongue, and thou
thoughtest wickedly that I am even such a one ' as thy'self : but
I will reprove thee, and set before thee the ' things that '
thou hast ' done.

22 O consider this ye that for'get ' God : lest I pluck you away and '
there be ' none to de'liver you.

23 Whoso offereth me thanks and praise, he ' honoureth ' me : and to
him that ordereth his conversation right will I ' shew the sal-'
vation of ' God.

PSALM 51

Vss 1-13

M. CAMIDGE

102

HAVE mercy upon me O God after ' thy great ' goodness : according to
the multitude of thy mercies ' do a'way mine of'fences.

2 Wash me throughly ' from my ' wickedness : and ' cleanse me '
from my ' sin.

3 For I ac'knowledge my ' faults : and my ' sin is ' ever be'fore me.

4 Against thee only have I sinned, and done this evil ' in thy ' sight :
that thou mightest be justified in thy saying, and ' clear when '
thou art ' judged.

5 Behold I was ' shapen in ' wickedness : and in ' sin hath my '
mother con'ceived me.

6 But lo, thou requirest truth in the ' inward ' parts : and shalt make
me to under'stand ' wisdom ' secretly.

7 Thou shalt purge me with hyssop, and ' I shall be ' clean : thou
shalt wash me, and ' I shall be ' whiter than ' snow.

8 Thou shalt make me hear of ' joy and ' gladness : that the bones
which thou hast ' broken ' may re'joice.

9 Turn thy face ' from my ' sins : and ' put out ' all my mis'deeds.

10 Make me a clean ' heart O ' God : and re'new a right ' spirit with-'
in me.

11 Cast me not away ' from thy ' presence : and take not thy ' holy '
Spirit ' from me.

12 O give me the comfort of thy ' help a'gain : and stablish me '
with thy ' free ' Spirit.

2nd 13 Then shall I teach thy ways ' unto the ' wicked : and sinners shall
Part   be con'verted ' unto ' thee.

Vss 14-end.   M. CAMIDGE

103

14 Deliver me from blood-guiltiness O God, thou that art the '
God of my ' health : and my ' tongue shall ' sing of thy '
righteousness.

15 Thou shalt open my ' lips O ' Lord : and my ' mouth shall '
shew thy ' praise.

16 For thou desirest no sacrifice ' else would I ' give it thee : but thou
delightest ' not in ' burnt'offerings.

17 The sacrifice of God is a ' troubled ' spirit : a broken and contrite
heart O God ' shalt thou ' not des'pise.

18 O be favourable and gracious ' unto ' Sion : build ' thou the '
walls of Je'rusalem.

19 Then shalt thou be pleased with the sacrifice of righteousness, with
the burnt-offerings ' and ob'lations : then shall they offer young '
bullocks up'on thine ' altar.

PSALM 52

T. S. DUPUIS

104

WHY boastest thou thy'self thou ' tyrant : that ' thou canst ' do ' mischief;

2 Whereas the ' goodness of ' God : en'dureth ' yet ' daily?

3 Thy tongue im'agineth ' wickedness : and with lies thou cuttest ' like a ' sharp ' rasor.

4 Thou hast loved unrighteousness ' more than ' goodness : and to talk of ' lies ' more than ' righteousness.

5 Thou hast loved to speak all words that ' may do ' hurt : O ' thou ' false ' tongue.

6 Therefore shall God destroy ' thee for ' ever : he shall take thee and pluck thee out of thy dwelling, and root thee ' out of the ' land of the ' living.

7 The righteous also shall see ' this and ' fear : and shall ' laugh ' him to ' scorn;

8 Lo this is the man that took not ' God for his ' strength : but trusted unto the multitude of his riches, and ' strengthened him-' self in his ' wickedness.

9 As for me I am like a green olive-tree in the ' house of ' God : my trust is in the tender mercy of ' God for ' ever and ' ever.

10 I will always give thanks unto thee for that ' thou hast ' done : and I will hope in thy Name for thy ' saints ' like it ' well.

DAY 10   EVENING
PSALM 53

W. CROSS

105

THE foolish body hath said ' in his ' heart : There ' is ' no ' God.

2 Corrupt are they, and become abominable ' in their ' wickedness : there is ' none that ' doeth ' good.

3 God looked down from heaven upon the ' children of ' men : to see
if there were any that would understand and ' seek ' after ' God.

4 But they are all gone out of the way, they are altogether be'come a-'
bominable : there is also none that doeth ' good ' no not ' one.

5 Are not they without understanding that ' work ' wickedness :
eating up my people as if they would eat bread? they ' have not '
called upon ' God.

6 They were afraid where ' no fear ' was : for God hath broken the
bones of him that besieged thee, thou hast put them to confusion,
because ' God ' hath des'pised them.

7 O that the salvation were given unto Israel ' out of ' Sion : O that
the Lord would deliver his ' people ' out of cap'tivity!

8 Then should ' Jacob re'joice : and Israel ' should be ' right ' glad.

PSALM 54

J. NARES

106

p   SAVE me O God for thy ' Name's ' sake : and a'venge me ' in thy '
strength.

2 Hear my ' prayer O ' God : and hearken ' unto the ' words of my '
mouth.

2nd Part   3 For strangers are risen ' up a'gainst me : and tyrants which have
not God before their eyes ' seek ' after my ' soul.

f   4 Behold ' God is my ' helper : the Lord is with ' them that up-'
hold my ' soul.

5 He shall reward evil ' unto mine ' enemies : destroy thou ' them in '
thy ' truth.

6 An offering of a free heart will I give thee, and praise thy ' Name O '
Lord : be'cause it ' is so ' comfortable.

7 For he hath delivered me out of ' all my ' trouble : and mine eye
hath seen his de'sire up'on mine ' enemies.

PSALM 55

J. GOSS from J. CLARKE

107

HEAR my ' prayer O ' God : and hide not thy'self from ' my pe'tition.

2 Take heed unto ' me and ' hear me : how I mourn in my ' prayer ' and am ' vexed.

3 The enemy crieth so, and the ungodly cometh ' on so ' fast : for they are minded to do me some mischief, so maliciously ' are they ' set a'gainst me.

4 My heart is dis'quieted with'in me : and the fear of ' death is ' fallen up'on me.

5 Fearfulness and trembling are ' come up'on me : and an horrible ' dread hath ' over'whelmed me.

6 And I said, O that I had ' wings like a ' dove : for then would I flee a'way and ' be at ' rest.

7 Lo then would I get me a'way far ' off : and re'main ' in the ' wilderness.

8 I would make ' haste to es'cape : because of the ' stormy ' wind and ' tempest.

9 Destroy their tongues O Lord ' and di'vide them : for I have spied un'righteousness and ' strife in the ' city.

10 Day and night they go about within the ' walls there'of : mischief also and ' sorrow are ' in the ' midst of it.

11 Wickedness ' is there'in : deceit and guile ' go not ' out of their ' streets.

12 For it is not an open enemy that hath done me ' this dis'honour : for ' then I ' could have ' borne it.

13 Neither was it mine adversary, that did magnify him'self a-' gainst me : for then peradventure I would have ' hid my'self ' from him.

14 But it was even thou ' my com'panion : my guide and mine ' own fa'miliar ' friend.

(2nd   15 We took sweet ' counsel to'gether : and walked in the ' house of '
Part)   God as ' friends.

[16 Let death come hastily upon them, and let them go down '
quick into ' hell : for wickedness is in their ' dwellings ' and a-'
mong them.]

17 As for me, I will ' call upon ' God : and the ' Lord ' shall ' save me.

18 In the evening and morning and at noon-day will I ' pray and that '
instantly : and ' he shall ' hear my ' voice.

19 It is he that hath delivered my soul in peace from the battle that '
was a'gainst me : for ' there were ' many ' with me.

20 Yea even God that endureth for ever shall hear me and ' bring them '
down : for they will not ' turn nor ' fear ' God.

21 He laid his hands upon such as be at ' peace with ' him : and he '
brake ' his ' convenant.

22 The words of his mouth were softer than butter, having ' war in his '
heart : his words were smoother than oil, and yet ' be they ' very '
swords.

23 O cast thy burden upon the Lord, and he shall ' nourish ' thee : and
shall not suffer the ' righteous to ' fall for ' ever.

24 And ' as for ' them : thou O God shalt bring them ' into the '
pit of de'struction.

2nd   25 The blood-thirsty and deceitful men shall not live out ' half their '
Part   days : nevertheless my trust shall ' be in ' thee O ' Lord.

DAY 11   MORNING

PSALM 56

W. BAYLEY

108

BE merciful unto me O God, for man goeth a'bout to de'vour me :
he is daily ' fighting and ' troubling ' me.

2 Mine enemies are daily in hand to ' swallow me ' up : for they be
many that fight against ' me O ' thou most ' Highest.

3 Nevertheless though I am ' sometime a'fraid : yet put ' I my '
trust in ' thee.

4 I will praise God be'cause of his ' word : I have put my trust in God,
and will not fear what ' flesh can ' do unto ' me.

93

W. BAYLEY

108

5 They daily mis'take my ' words : all that they imagine ' is to '
do me ' evil.

6 They hold all together and ' keep themselves ' close : and mark my
steps, when they lay ' wait ' for my ' soul.

7 Shall they escape ' for their ' wickedness : thou O God in thy
dis'pleasure shalt ' cast them ' down.

8 Thou tellest my flittings, put my tears ' into thy ' bottle : are not
these things ' noted ' in thy ' book?

2nd Part   9 Whensoever I call upon thee, then shall mine enemies be ' put to '
flight : this I know, for ' God is ' on my ' side.

10 In God's word will ' I re'joice : in the ' Lord's word ' will I '
comfort me.

11 Yea in God have I ' put my ' trust : I will not be afraid what '
man can ' do unto ' me.

12 Unto thee O God will I ' pay my ' vows : unto ' thee will ' I give '
thanks.

13 For thou hast delivered my soul from death and my ' feet from '
falling : that I may walk before ' God in the ' light of the ' living.

PSALM 57

Vss 1-5 and 7   W. FELTON

109

Vss 6 and 8 - end   ANON

110   Verses 6 and 12 unison

Bᴇ merciful unto me O God, be merciful unto me, for my soul '
trusteth in ' thee : and under the shadow of thy wings shall be
my refuge, until this ' tyranny be ' over'past.

2 I will call unto the ' most high ' God : even unto the God that shall
perform the cause ' which I ' have in ' hand.

3 He shall ' send from ' heaven : and save me from the reproof of '
   him that would ' eat me ' up.

4 God shall send forth his ' mercy and ' truth : my ' soul is a'mong '
   lions.

5 And I lie even among the children of men that are ' set on ' fire :
   whose teeth are spears and arrows, and their ' tongue a ' sharp '
   sword.

Unison
   f   6 Set up thyself O God a'bove the ' heavens : and thy glory a'bove '
            all the ' earth.

   p   7 They have laid a net for my feet, and press-ed ' down my ' soul :
            they have digged a pit before me, and are fallen into the '
            midst of ' it them'selves.

   f   8 My heart is fixed O God my ' heart is ' fixed : I will ' sing and ' give '
            praise.

         9 Awake up my glory, awake ' lute and ' harp : I myself ' will a-'
            wake right ' early.

        10 I will give thanks unto thee O Lord a'mong the ' people : and I will
            sing unto ' thee a'mong the ' nations.

        11 For the greatness of thy mercy reacheth ' unto the ' heavens : and
            thy ' truth ' unto the ' clouds.

Unison 12 Set up thyself O God a'bove the ' heavens : and thy glory a'bove '
            all the ' earth.

[PSALM 58

W. HORSLEY

11

ARE your minds set upon righteousness O ye ' congre'gation : and do
    ye judge the thing that is right ' O ye ' sons of ' men?

2 Yea ye imagine mischief in your heart up'on the ' earth : and your '
   hands ' deal with ' wickedness.

3 The ungodly are froward, even from their ' mother's ' womb : as
   soon as they are born, they go a'stray and ' speak ' lies.

4 They are as venomous as the ' poison of a ' serpent : even like the
   deaf ' adder that ' stoppeth her ' ears;

5 Which refuseth to hear the ' voice of the ' charmer : charm he never ' so ' wisely.

6 Break their teeth O God in their mouths, smite the jaw-bones of the lions O ' Lord : let them fall away like water that runneth apace and when they shoot their arrows ' let them be ' rooted ' out.

7 Let them consume away like a snail, and be like the untimely fruit of a ' woman : and ' let them not ' see the ' sun.

8 Or ever your pots be made ' hot with ' thorns : so let indignation vex him, ' even as a ' thing that is ' raw.

9 The righteous shall rejoice when he ' seeth the ' vengeance : he shall wash his footsteps in the ' blood of ' the un'godly.

10 So that a man shall say, Verily there is a re'ward for the ' righteous doubtless there is a ' God that ' judgeth the ' earth.]

DAY 11   EVENING

PSALM 59

or

DELIVER me from mine ' enemies O ' God : defend me from them that rise ' up a'gainst me.

2 O deliver me from the ' wicked ' doers : and save me ' from the ' blood-thirsty ' men.

3 For lo they lie waiting ' for my ' soul : the mighty men are gathered against me, without any offence or ' fault of ' me O ' Lord.

4 They run and prepare themselves with'out my ' fault : arise thou therefore to ' help me ' and be'hold.

5 Stand up O Lord God of hosts thou God of Israel, to visit ' all the ' heathen : and be not merciful unto them that offend ' of ma'licious ' wickedness.

6 They go to and fro ' in the ' evening : they grin like a dog, and ' run a'bout through the ' city.

7 Behold they speak with their mouth, and swords are ' in their ' lips : for ' who ' doth ' hear?

8 But thou O Lord shalt have them ' in de'rision : and thou shalt laugh ' all the ' heathen to ' scorn.

9 My strength will I ascribe ' unto ' thee : for ' thou art the ' God of my ' refuge.

10 God sheweth me his ' goodness ' plenteously : and God shall let me see my de'sire up'on mine ' enemies.

11 Slay them not lest my ' people for'get it : but scatter them abroad among the people, and put them down O ' Lord ' our de'fence.

12 For the sin of their mouth and for the words of their lips, they shall be taken ' in their ' pride : and why?, their preaching ' is of ' cursing and ' lies.

13 Consume them in thy wrath, consume them that ' they may ' perish : and know that it is God that ruleth in Jacob and ' unto the ' ends of the ' world.

14 And in the evening they ' will re'turn : grin like a dog and will ' go a'bout the ' city.

15 They will run here and ' there for ' meat : and grudge ' if they ' be not ' satisfied.

16 As for me I will sing of thy power, and will praise thy mercy be'times in the ' morning : for thou hast been my defence and ' refuge in the ' day of my ' trouble.

2nd   17 Unto thee O my strength ' will I ' sing : for thou O God art my '
Part   refuge · and my ' merciful ' God.

PSALM 60

114

p   O GOD thou has cast us out and scattered ' us a'broad : thou hast also been displeased, O turn thee ' unto ' us a'gain.

2 Thou hast moved the ' land and di'vided it : heal the ' sores thereof ' for it ' shaketh.

3 Thou hast shewed thy people ' heavy ' things : thou hast given us a ' drink of ' deadly ' wine.

4 Thou hast given a token for ' such as ' fear thee : that they may ' triumph be'cause of the ' truth.

5 Therefore were thy be'loved de'livered : help me with ' thy right ' hand and ' hear me.

115

f   6 God hath spoken in his holiness, I will rejoice and di'vide ' Sichem and mete ' out the ' valley of ' Succoth.

7 Gilead is mine and Ma'nasses is ' mine : Ephraim also is the strength of my head, ' Judah ' is my ' law-giver;

8 Moab is my wash-pot, over Edom will I cast ' out my ' shoe Philistia ' be thou ' glad of ' me.

9 Who will lead me into the ' strong ' city : who will ' bring me ' into Edom?

10 Hast not thou cast us ' out O ' God : wilt not thou O ' God go out with our ' hosts?

11 O be thou our ' help in ' trouble : for ' vain is the ' help of ' man.

12 Through God will we ' do great ' acts : for it is he that ' shall tread down our ' enemies.

PSALM 61

S. ELVEY

16

mf   HEAR my ' crying O ' God : give ' ear ' unto my ' prayer.

   2 From the ends of the earth will I ' call upon ' thee : when my ' heart ' is in ' heaviness.

   3 O set me up upon the rock that is ' higher than ' I : for thou hast been my hope, and a strong tower for ' me a'gainst the ' enemy.

   4 I will dwell in thy ' tabernacle for ' ever : and my trust shall be under the ' covering ' of thy ' wings.

f   5 For thou O Lord hast ' heard my de'sires : and hast given an heritage unto ' those that ' fear thy ' Name.

   6 Thou shalt grant the ' King a long ' life : that his years may endure through'out all ' gene'rations.

   7 He shall dwell before ' God for ' ever : O prepare thy loving mercy and ' faithfulness that ' they may pre'serve him.

   8 So will I alway sing praise ' unto thy ' Name : that I may ' daily per'form my ' vows.

DAY 12   MORNING

PSALM 62

W. BOYCE

17

MY soul truly waiteth ' still upon ' God : for of him ' cometh ' my sal'vation.

   2 He verily is my strength and ' my sal'vation : he is my defence, so that I ' shall not ' greatly ' fall.

99

3 How long will ye imagine mischief against ' every ' man : ye shall be slain all the sort of you, yea   as a tottering wall shall ye be and ' like a ' broken ' hedge.

4 Their device is only how to put him out whom ' God will ex'alt their delight is in lies, they give good words with their ' mouth but ' curse with their ' heart.

5 Nevertheless my soul wait thou ' still upon ' God : for my ' hope is in ' him.

6 He truly is my strength and ' my sal'vation : he is my defence so that I ' shall not ' fall.

7 In God is my ' health and my ' glory : the rock of my might, and in God is ' my ' trust.

8 O put your trust in him ' alway ye ' people : pour out your hearts before him, for ' God is ' our ' hope.

9 As for the children of men ' they are but ' vanity : the children of men are deceitful upon the weights, they are altogether lighter than ' vanity it'self.

10 O trust not in wrong and robbery, give not yourselves ' unto vanity : if riches increase ' set not your ' heart up'on them.

11 God spake once, and twice I have also ' heard the ' same : that power be'longeth ' unto ' God;

12 And that thou ' Lord art ' merciful : for thou rewardest every man ac'cording ' to his ' work.

PSALM 63

O GOD ' thou art my ' God : early ' will I ' seek ' thee.

2 My soul thirsteth for thee, my flesh also longeth ' after ' thee : in barren and dry land ' where no ' water ' is.

3 Thus have I looked for ' thee in ' holiness : that I might be'hold thy ' power and ' glory.

4 For thy loving-kindness is better than the ' life it'self : my ' lips shall ' praise ' thee.

5 As long as I live will I magnify thee ' on this ' manner : and lift up my ' hands in ' thy ' Name.

6 My soul shall be satisfied, even as it were with ' marrow and ' fatness : when my mouth praiseth ' thee with ' joyful ' lips.

7 Have I not remembered thee ' in my ' bed : and thought upon ' thee when ' I was ' waking?

8 Because thou hast ' been my ' helper : therefore under the shadow of thy ' wings will ' I re'joice.

9 My soul ' hangeth up'on thee : thy ' right hand ' hath up-' holden me.

10 These also that seek the ' hurt of my ' soul : they shall ' go ' under the ' earth.

11 Let them fall upon the ' edge of the ' sword : that they may ' be a ' portion for ' foxes.

12 But the King shall rejoice in God, all they also that swear by him shall ' be com'mended : for the mouth of them that speak ' lies ' shall be ' stopped.

PSALM 64

J. NARES

119

HEAR my voice O God ' in my ' prayer : preserve my ' life from ' fear of the ' enemy.

2 Hide me from the gathering together ' of the ' froward : and from the insur'rection of ' wicked ' doers;

3 Who have whet their tongue ' like a ' sword : and shoot out their arrows ' even ' bitter ' words;

4 That they may privily shoot at ' him that is ' perfect : suddenly do they ' hit him and ' fear ' not.

J. NARES

119

5 They encourage them'selves in ' mischief : and commune among themselves how they may lay snares, and ' say that ' no man shall ' see them.

6 They imagine ' wickedness and ' practise it : that they keep secret among themselves, every man ' in the ' deep of his ' heart.

7 But God shall suddenly shoot at them with a ' swift ' arrow : that ' they ' shall be ' wounded.

8 Yea their own tongues shall ' make them ' fall : insomuch that whoso ' seeth them shall ' laugh them to ' scorn.

9 And all men that see it shall say, This hath ' God ' done : for they shall perceive that ' it is ' his ' work.

f 10 The righteous shall rejoice in the Lord and put his ' trust in ' him : and all they that are ' true of ' heart shall be ' glad.

DAY 12 EVENING

PSALM 65

G. M. GARRET

120

THOU O God art ' praised in ' Sion : and unto thee shall the vow be per'form-ed ' in Je'rusalem.

2 Thou that ' hearest the ' prayer : unto ' thee shall ' all flesh ' come

3 My misdeeds pre'vail a'gainst me : O be thou ' merciful ' unto our sins.

4 Blessed is the man whom thou choosest and receivest ' unto ' thee : he shall dwell in thy court, and shall be satisfied with the pleasures of thy house, even ' of thy ' holy ' temple.

5 Thou shalt shew us wonderful things in thy righteousness, O God of ' our sal'vation : thou that art the hope of all the ends of the earth, and of them that re'main in the ' broad ' sea.

6 Who in his strength setteth ' fast the ' mountains : and is ' girded a'bout with ' power.

7 Who stilleth the ' raging · of the ' sea : and the noise of his waves and the ' madness ' of the ' people.

8 They also that dwell in the uttermost parts of the earth shall be afraid ' at thy ' tokens : thou that makest the outgoings of the ' morning and ' evening to ' praise thee.

9 Thou visitest the ' earth and ' blessest it : thou ' makest it ' very ' plenteous.

10 The river of God is ' full of ' water : thou preparest their corn, for so thou pro'videst ' for the ' earth.

11 Thou waterest her furrows, thou sendest rain into the little ' valleys there'of : thou makest it soft with the drops of rain, and ' blessest the ' increase ' of it.

12 Thou crownest the year ' with thy ' goodness : and thy ' clouds ' drop ' fatness.

13 They shall drop upon the ' dwellings · of the ' wilderness : and the little hills shall re'joice on ' every ' side.

14 The folds shall be ' full of ' sheep : the valleys also shall stand so thick with corn that ' they shall ' laugh and ' sing.

PSALM 66

G. J. ELVEY

O BE joyful in God ' all ye ' lands : sing praises unto the honour of his Name, make his ' praise ' to be ' glorious.

2 Say unto God, O how wonderful art thou ' in thy ' works : through the greatness of thy power shall thine enemies be found ' liars ' unto ' thee.

G. J. ELVEY

121

3 For all the ' world shall ' worship thee : sing of ' thee and ' praise thy ' Name.

4 O come hither and behold the ' works of ' God : how wonderful he is in his doing ' toward the ' children of ' men.

5 He turned the sea into ' dry ' land : so that they went through the water on foot, there did ' we re'joice there'of.

6 He ruleth with his power for ever, his eyes be'hold the ' people : and such as will not believe, shall not be ' able to ex'alt them'selves.

7 O praise our ' God ye ' people : and make the ' voice of his praise to be ' heard;

8 Who holdeth our ' soul in ' life : and suffereth ' not our ' feet to slip.

9 For thou O ' God hast ' proved us : thou also hast tried us ' like as silver is ' tried.

10 Thou broughtest us ' into the ' snare : and laidest ' trouble up- on our ' loins.

11 Thou sufferedst men to ride ' over our ' heads : we went through fire and water, and thou broughtest us out ' into a ' wealthy place.

12 I will go into thine house with ' burnt'offerings : and will pay thee my vows, which I promised with my lips and spake with my mouth ' when I ' was in ' trouble.

13 I will offer unto thee fat burnt-sacrifices, with the ' incense of rams : I will ' offer ' bullocks and ' goats.

14 O come hither and hearken, all ye that ' fear ' God : and I will tell you what ' he hath ' done for my ' soul.

15 I called unto him ' with my ' mouth : and gave him ' praises with my ' tongue.

16 If I incline unto wickedness ' with mine ' heart : the ' Lord will not ' hear me.

17 But ' God hath ' heard me : and con'sidered the ' voice of my prayer.

18 Praised be God who hath not cast ' out my ' prayer : nor turned his ' mercy ' from me.

PSALM 67

122

God be merciful unto ' us and ' bless us : and shew us the light of his
countenance, and be ' merciful ' unto ' us :

2 That thy way may be ' known upon ' earth : thy saving '
health a'mong all ' nations.

Unison 3 Let the people ' praise thee O ' God : yea let ' all the ' people '
praise thee.

4 O let the nations re'joice and be ' glad : for thou shalt judge the folk
righteously, and govern the ' nations up'on ' earth.

Unison 5 Let the people ' praise thee O ' God : let ' all the ' people '
praise thee.

6 Then shall the earth bring ' forth her ' increase : and God even our
own ' God shall ' give us his ' blessing.

2nd Pt. 7 God ' shall ' bless us : and all the ' ends of the ' world shall '
fear him.

DAY 13   MORNING

PSALM 68

123

Let God arise and let his ' enemies be ' scattered : let them also that '
hate him ' flee be'fore him.

2 Like as the smoke vanisheth, so shalt thou ' drive them a'way : and
like as wax melteth at the fire, so let the ungodly ' perish at the '
presence of ' God.

J. GOSS

123

3 But let the righteous be glad and re'joice before ' God : let them '
  also be ' merry and ' joyful.

4 O sing unto God and sing praises ' unto his ' Name : magnify him
  that rideth upon the heavens as it were upon an horse, praise him
  in his Name JAH ' and re'joice be'fore him.

5 He is a father of the fatherless, and defendeth the ' cause of the '
  widows : even God in his ' holy ' habi'tation.

6 He is the God that maketh men to be of one mind in an house, and
  bringeth the prisoners ' out of cap'tivity : but letteth the '
  runagates con'tinue in ' scarceness.

7 O God when thou wentest forth be'fore the ' people : when thou '
  wentest ' through the ' wilderness;

8 The earth shook and the heavens dropped, at the ' presence of '
  God : even as Sinai also was moved at the presence of God who '
  is the ' God of ' Israel.

9 Thou O God sentest a gracious rain upon ' thine in'heritance : and
  re'freshedst it ' when it was ' weary.

10 Thy congregation shall ' dwell there'in : for thou O God hast of thy
   goodness pre'par-ed ' for the ' poor.

11 The Lord ' gave the ' word : great was the ' company ' of the '
   preachers.

12 Kings with their armies did flee and ' were dis'comfited : and they
   of the ' household di'vided the ' spoil.

13 Though ye have lien among the pots, yet shall ye be as the '
   wings of a ' dove : that is covered with silver wings ' and her '
   feathers like ' gold.

14 When the Almighty scattered ' kings for their ' sake : then were
   they as ' white as ' snow in ' Salmon.

15 As the hill of Basan ' so is ' God's hill : even an high hill ' as the '
   hill of ' Basan.

16 Why hop ye so ye high hills? this is God's hill in the which it pleaseth ' him to ' dwell : yea the Lord will a'bide in ' it for ' ever.

17 The chariots of God are twenty thousand, even ' thousands of ' angels : and the Lord is among them, as in the ' holy ' place of ' Sinai.

18 Thou art gone up on high, thou hast led captivity captive, and received ' gifts for ' men : yea even for thine enemies, that the Lord ' God might ' dwell a'mong them.

19 Praised be the ' Lord ' daily : even the God who helpeth us, and ' poureth his ' benefits up'on us.

20 He is our God, even the God of whom ' cometh sal'vation : God is the Lord by ' whom we es'cape ' death.

[21 God shall wound the ' head of his ' enemies : and the hairy scalp of such a one as ' goeth on ' still in his ' wickedness.

22 The Lord hath said, I will bring my people again as I ' did from ' Basan : mine own will I bring again, as I did sometime ' from the ' deep of the ' sea.

2nd 23 That thy foot may be dipped in the ' blood of thine ' enemies : and
Part   that the tongue of thy ' dogs may be ' red through the ' same.]

24

25

24 It is well seen O God ' how thou ' goest : how thou my God and King ' goest ' in the ' sanctuary.

25 The singers go before, the minstrels ' follow ' after : in the midst are the damsels ' playing ' with the ' timbrels.

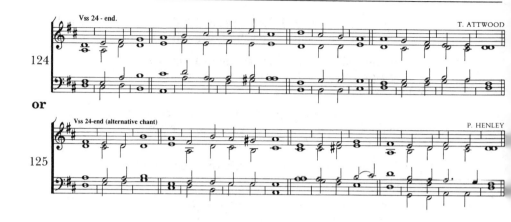

or

26 Give thanks O Israel unto God the Lord in the ' congre'gations :
from the ' ground ' of the ' heart.

27 There is little Benjamin their ruler, and the princes of ' Judah their '
counsel : the princes of ' Zabulon · and the ' princes of ' Nephthali.

28 Thy God hath sent forth ' strength for ' thee : stablish the thing O
God that ' thou hast ' wrought in ' us,

29 For thy temple's sake ' at Je'rusalem : so shall kings bring '
presents ' unto ' thee.

30 When the company of the spear-men and multitude of the mighty,
are scattered abroad among the beasts of the people, so that they
humbly bring ' pieces of ' silver : and when he hath scattered the
people ' that de'light in ' war;

31 Then shall the princes come ' out of ' Egypt : the Morians' land
shall soon stretch ' out her ' hands · unto ' God.

32 Sing unto God O ye ' kingdoms of the ' earth : O sing ' praises '
unto the ' Lord;

33 Who sitteth in the heavens over all ' from the be'ginning : lo he
doth send out his voice, yea and ' that a ' mighty ' voice.

34 Ascribe ye the power to God ' over ' Israel : his worship and '
strength is ' in the ' clouds.

35 O God wonderful art thou in thy ' holy ' places : even the God of
Israel, he will give strength and power unto his people, ' blessed '
be ' God.

DAY 13 EVENING

PSALM 69

26

SAVE ' me O ' God : for the waters are come in ' even ' unto my ' soul.

2 I stick fast in the deep mire ' where no ' ground is : I am come into deep waters ' so that the ' floods run ' over me.

3 I am weary of crying, my ' throat is ' dry : my sight faileth me for ' waiting so ' long upon my ' God.

4 They that hate me without a cause are more than the ' hairs of my ' head : they that are mine enemies, and would de'stroy me ' guiltless are ' mighty.

5 I paid them the things that I ' never ' took : God thou knowest my simpleness, and my faults ' are not ' hid from ' thee.

6 Let not them that trust in thee O Lord God of hosts, be ashamed for ' my ' cause : let not those that seek thee be confounded through me, O ' Lord ' God of ' Israel.

7 And why?, for thy sake have I ' suffered re'proof : shame hath ' covered ' my ' face.

8 I am become a stranger ' unto my ' brethren : even an alien ' unto my ' mother's ' children.

9 For the zeal of thine house hath ' even ' eaten me : and the rebukes of them that rebuked ' thee are ' fallen up'on me.

10 I wept and chastened my'self with ' fasting : and that was ' turned to ' my re'proof.

11 I put on ' sackcloth ' also : and they ' jested up'on ' me.

12 They that sit in the gate ' speak a'gainst me : and the ' drunkards make ' songs up'on me.

Change to Chant 127 overleaf

127

13 But Lord I make my prayer ' unto ' thee : in ' an ac'ceptable ' time.

14 Hear me O God in the multitude ' of thy ' mercy : even in the ' truth of ' thy sal'vation.

15 Take me out of the mire ' that I ' sink not : O let me be delivered from them that hate me, and ' out of the ' deep ' waters.

16 Let not the water-flood drown me, neither let the deep ' swallow me ' up : and let not the pit ' shut her ' mouth up'on me.

17 Hear me O Lord, for thy loving'kindness is ' comfortable : turn thee unto me according to the ' multitude ' of thy ' mercies.

18 And hide not thy face from thy servant for ' I am in ' trouble : O ' haste ' thee and ' hear me.

19 Draw nigh unto my ' soul and ' save it : O de'liver me be-' cause of mine ' enemies.

20 Thou hast known my reproof my shame and ' my dis'honour : mine adversaries are ' all in ' thy ' sight.

21 Thy rebuke hath broken my heart, I am ' full of ' heaviness : I looked for some to have pity on me, but there was no man, neither ' found I ' any to ' comfort me.

22 They gave me ' gall to ' eat : and when I was thirsty they ' gave me ' vinegar to ' drink.

126

[23 Let their table be made a snare to take them'selves with'al : and let the things that should have been for their wealth, be unto ' them an oc'casion of ' falling.

110

24 Let their eyes be blinded ' that they ' see not : and ever ' bow thou ' down their ' backs.

25 Pour out thine indig'nation up'on them : and let thy ' wrathful dis'pleasure take ' hold of them.

26 Let their habi'tation be ' void : and ' no man to ' dwell in their ' tents.

27 For they persecute him whom ' thou hast ' smitten : and they talk how they may vex ' them whom ' thou hast ' wounded.

28 Let them fall from one wickedness ' to an'other : and ' not come ' into thy ' righteousness.

2nd 29 Let them be wiped out of the ' book of the ' living : and not be '
Part   written a'mong the ' righteous.]

30 As for me, when I am ' poor and in ' heaviness : thy help O ' God shall ' lift me ' up.

31 I will praise the Name of ' God · with a ' song : and ' magni-' fy it with ' thanksgiving.

32 This also shall ' please the ' Lord : better than a bullock ' that hath ' horns and ' hoofs.

33 The humble shall consider this ' and be ' glad : seek ye after God ' and your ' soul shall ' live.

34 For the Lord ' heareth the ' poor : and des'piseth ' not his ' prisoners.

35 Let heaven and ' earth ' praise him : the sea and ' all that ' moveth there'in.

36 For God will save Sion, and build the ' cities of ' Judah : that men may dwell there and ' have it ' in pos'session.

37 The posterity also of his servants ' shall in'herit it : and they that love his ' Name shall ' dwell there'in.

111

PSALM 70

128

HASTE thee O God ' to de'liver me : make ' haste to ' help me O ' Lord.

2 Let them be ashamed and confounded that seek ' after my ' soul :
let them be turned backward and put to con'fusion that ' wish me '
evil.

3 Let them for their reward be soon ' brought to ' shame : that cry '
over me ' There ' there.

129

4 But let all those that seek thee be joyful and ' glad in ' thee : and let
all such as delight in thy salvation say ' alway The ' Lord be '
praised.

5 As for me I am ' poor and in ' misery : haste thee ' unto ' me O '
God.

6 Thou art my helper and ' my re'deemer : O ' Lord make ' no long '
tarrying.

DAY 14   MORNING

PSALM 71

130

IN thee O Lord have I put my trust, let me never be ' put to con'fusion :
but rid me and deliver me in thy righteousness, incline thine ear '
unto ' me and ' save me.

2 Be thou my strong hold whereunto I may ' alway re'sort : thou hast
promised to help me, for thou art my house of de'fence and ' my '
castle.

3 Deliver me O my God out of the ' hand of · the un'godly : out of the hand of the un'righteous and ' cruel ' man.

4 For thou O Lord God art the ' thing that I ' long for : thou art my hope ' even ' from my ' youth.

5 Through thee have I been holden up ever since ' I was ' born : thou art he that took me out of my mother's womb, my praise ' shall be ' always of ' thee.

6 I am become as it were a monster ' unto ' many : but my ' sure ' trust is in ' thee.

7 O let my mouth be ' filled with thy ' praise : that I may sing of thy glory and ' honour ' all the day ' long.

8 Cast me not away in the ' time of ' age : forsake me not ' when my ' strength ' faileth me.

9 For mine enemies speak against me, and they that lay wait for my soul take their counsel to'gether ' saying : God hath forsaken him, persecute him and take him, for ' there is ' none to de-' liver him.

10 Go not far from ' me O ' God : my God ' haste ' thee to ' help me.

11 Let them be confounded and perish that are a'gainst my ' soul : let them be covered with shame and dishonour that ' seek to ' do me ' evil.

12 As for me I will patiently a'bide ' alway : and will ' praise thee ' more and ' more.

13 My mouth shall daily speak of thy righteousness ' and sal'vation : for I ' know no ' end there'of.

14 I will go forth in the strength of the ' Lord ' God : and will make mention of ' thy ' righteousness ' only.

15 Thou O God hast taught me from my youth up ' until ' now : therefore will I ' tell of thy ' wondrous ' works.

16 Forsake me not O God in mine old age, when I am ' gray'headed : until I have shewed thy strength unto this generation, and thy power to all ' them that are ' yet for to ' come.

W. H. GRAY

130

17 Thy righteousness O God is ' very ' high : and great things are they
 that thou hast done, O God ' who is ' like unto ' thee?

18 O what great troubles and adversities hast thou shewed me, and
 yet didst thou ' turn and re'fresh me : yea and broughtest me
 from the ' deep of the ' earth a'gain.

19 Thou hast brought me to ' great ' honour : and comforted ' me on '
 every ' side.

20 Therefore will I praise thee and thy faithfulness O God, playing
 upon an ' instrument of ' musick : unto thee will I sing upon the
 harp, O thou ' Holy ' One of ' Israel.

21 My lips will be fain when I sing ' unto ' thee : and so will my soul '
 whom thou ' hast de'livered.

22 My tongue also shall talk of thy righteousness ' all the day ' long :
 for they are confounded and brought unto shame that ' seek to '
 do me ' evil.

PSALM 72

T. NORRIS

131

Give the King thy ' judgements O ' God : and thy righteousness '
 unto the ' King's ' son.

* 2 Then shall he judge thy people ac'cording ' unto ' right : ' and de-' fend the ' poor.

3 The mountains also ' shall bring ' peace : and the little hills ' righteousness ' unto the ' people.

4 He shall keep the simple folk ' by their ' right : defend the children of the poor and ' punish the ' wrong'doer.

5 They shall fear thee as long as the sun and ' moon en'dureth : from one gene'ration ' to an'other.

6 He shall come down like the rain into a ' fleece of ' wool : even as the ' drops that ' water the ' earth.

2nd Part 7 In his time shall the ' righteous ' flourish : yea and abundance of peace so ' long as the ' moon en'dureth.

8 His dominion shall be also from the one ' sea to the ' other : and from the flood ' unto the ' world's ' end.

9 They that dwell in the wilderness shall ' kneel be'fore him : his ' enemies shall ' lick the ' dust.

10 The kings of Tharsis and of the isles ' shall give ' presents : the kings of Arabia and ' Saba ' shall bring ' gifts.

11 All kings shall fall ' down be'fore him : all ' nations shall ' do him ' service.

12 For he shall deliver the poor ' when he ' crieth : the needy also and ' him that ' hath no ' helper.

13 He shall be favourable to the ' simple and ' needy : and shall pre'serve the ' souls of the ' poor.

14 He shall deliver their souls from ' falsehood and ' wrong : and dear shall their ' blood be ' in his ' sight.

15 He shall live, and unto him shall be given of the ' gold of A'rabia : prayer shall be made ever unto him and ' daily shall ' he be ' praised.

2 Then shall he judge thy people according ' unto ' right : and de'fend ' the ' poor.

16 There shall be an heap of corn in the earth, high up'on the ' hills :
his fruit shall shake like Libanus, and shall be green in the city
like ' grass up'on the ' earth.

17 His Name shall endure for ever, his Name shall remain under the
sun a'mong the pos'terities : which shall be blessed through him,
and ' all the ' heathen shall ' praise him.

18 Blessed be the Lord God, even the ' God of ' Israel : which only '
doeth ' wondrous ' things;

19 And blessed be the Name of his ' majesty for ' ever : and all the
earth shall be filled with his majesty. ' Amen ' A'men.

DAY 14   EVENING

PSALM 73

TRULY God is loving ' unto ' Israel : even unto such as ' are of a ' clean '
heart.

2 Nevertheless my feet were ' almost ' gone : my ' treadings had '
well-nigh ' slipt.

3 And why?, I was grieved ' at the ' wicked : I do also see the un-'
godly in ' such pros'perity.

116

* 4 For they are ' in no ' peril of ' death : ' but are ' lusty and ' strong.

5 They come in no mis'fortune like ' other folk : neither ' are they ' plagued like ' other men.

6 And this is the cause that they are so ' holden with ' pride : and ' over'whelmed with ' cruelty.

7 Their eyes ' swell with ' fatness : and they do ' even ' what they ' lust.

8 They corrupt other, and speak of ' wicked ' blasphemy : their talking is a'gainst the ' most ' High.

9 For they stretch forth their mouth ' unto the ' heaven : and their tongue ' goeth ' through the ' world.

10 Therefore fall the ' people ' unto them : and thereout ' suck they no ' small ad'vantage.

11 Tush say they, how should ' God per'ceive it : is there knowledge ' in the ' most ' High?

12 Lo these are the ungodly, these prosper in the world, and these have riches ' in pos'session : and I said, Then have I cleansed my heart in vain and ' washed mine ' hands in ' innocency.

13 All the day long have ' I been ' punished : and ' chastened ' every ' morning.

14 Yea and I had almost said ' even as ' they : but lo then I should have condemned the gene'ration ' of thy ' children.

15 Then thought I to under'stand ' this : but it ' was too ' hard for ' me,

16 Until I went into the ' sanctuary of ' God : then under'stood I the ' end of ' these men;

17 Namely how thou dost set them in ' slippery ' places : and ' castest them ' down and de'stroyest them.

18 O how suddenly do ' they con'sume : perish and ' come to a ' fearful ' end!

4 For they are in no ' peril of ' death : but are ' lusty ' and ' strong.

J. TURLE

132

19 Yea even like as a dream ' when one a'waketh : so shalt thou make their image to ' vanish ' out of the ' city.

20 Thus my ' heart was ' grieved : and it went ' even ' through my ' reins.

2nd 21 So foolish was ' I and ' ignorant : even as it ' were a ' beast be-'
Part　　fore thee.

22 Nevertheless I am ' alway by ' thee : for thou hast holden me ' by my ' right ' hand.

23 Thou shalt guide me ' with thy ' counsel : and after ' that re-'ceive me with ' glory.

24 Whom have I in ' heaven but ' thee : and there is none upon earth that I de'sire in com'parison of ' thee.

25 My flesh and my ' heart ' faileth : but God is the strength of my heart ' and my ' portion for ' ever.

26 For lo they that forsake ' thee shall ' perish : thou hast destroyed all them that com'mit forni'cation a'gainst thee.

27 But it is good for me to hold me fast by God, to put my trust in the ' Lord ' God : and to speak of all thy works in the ' gates of the ' daughter of ' Sion.

PSALM 74

J. T. HARRIS

133

O GOD wherefore art thou absent from ' us so ' long : why is thy wrath so hot a'gainst the ' sheep of thy ' pasture?

2 O think upon thy ' congre'gation : whom thou hast purchased ' and re'deemed of ' old.

118

3 Think upon the tribe of ' thine in'heritance : and mount ' Sion where'in thou hast ' dwelt.

4 Lift up thy feet, that thou mayest utterly destroy ' every ' enemy : which hath done ' evil ' in thy ' sanctuary.

5 Thine adversaries roar in the midst of thy ' congre'gations : and set ' up their ' banners for ' tokens.

6 He that hewed timber afore out of the ' thick ' trees : was known to ' bring it to an ' excellent ' work.

7 But now they break down all the carved ' work there'of : with ' axes ' and ' hammers.

8 They have set fire upon thy ' holy ' places : and have defiled the dwelling-place of thy Name ' even ' unto the ' ground.

9 Yea they said in their hearts, Let us make havock of them ' alto'gether : thus have they burnt up all the ' houses of ' God in the ' land.

10 We see not our tokens, there is not one ' prophet ' more : no not one is there among us, that under'standeth ' any ' more.

11 O God how long shall the adversary do ' this dis'honour : how long shall the enemy blas'pheme thy ' Name for ' ever?

12 Why withdrawest ' thou thy ' hand : why pluckest thou not thy right hand out of thy bosom ' to con'sume the ' enemy?

13 For God is my ' King of ' old : the help that is done upon earth he ' doeth ' it him'self.

14 Thou didst divide the sea ' through thy ' power : thou brakest the heads of the ' dragons ' in the ' waters.

15 Thou smotest the heads of Le'viathan in ' pieces : and gavest him to be meat for the ' people ' in the ' wilderness.

16 Thou broughtest out fountains and waters out of the ' hard ' rocks : thou ' driedst up ' mighty ' waters.

17 The day is thine and the ' night is ' thine : thou hast pre'pared the ' light and the ' sun.

18 Thou hast set all the ' borders · of the ' earth : thou ' hast made ' summer and ' winter.

19 Remember this O Lord, how the enemy ' hath re'buked : and how the foolish people ' hath blas'phemed thy ' Name.

20 O deliver not the soul of thy turtle-dove, unto the multitude ' of the ' enemies : and forget not the congre'gation · of the ' poor for ' ever.

J. T. HARRIS

133

21 Look up'on the ' covenant : for all the earth is full of darkness and ' cruel ' habi'tations.

22 O let not the simple go a'way a'shamed : but let the poor and needy give ' praise ' unto thy ' Name.

23 Arise O God maintain thine ' own ' cause : remember how the foolish man blas'phemeth ' thee ' daily.

24 Forget not the ' voice of thine ' enemies : the presumption of them that hate thee increaseth ' ever ' more and ' more.

DAY 15   MORNING

PSALM 75

W. H. HAVERGAL

134

UNTO thee O God do ' we give ' thanks : yea unto ' thee do ' we give ' thanks.

2 Thy Name also ' is so ' nigh : and that do thy ' wondrous ' works de'clare.

3 When I receive the ' congre'gation : I shall judge ac'cording ' unto ' right.

4 The earth is weak, and all the in'habiters there'of : I bear ' up the ' pillars ' of it.

5 I said unto the fools, Deal ' not so ' madly : and to the ungodly, ' Set not ' up your ' horn.

6 Set not up your ' horn on ' high : and ' speak not ' with a stiff ' neck.

* 7 For promotion cometh neither ' from the ' east nor ' from the ' west : nor ' yet from the ' south.

8 And why? ' God is the ' Judge : he putteth down one and ' setteth ' up an'other.

9 For in the hand of the Lord there is a cup and the ' wine is ' red : it is full mixed, and he ' poureth ' out of the ' same.

10 As for the ' dregs there'of : all the ungodly of the earth shall ' drink them and ' suck them ' out.

11 But I will talk of the ' God of ' Jacob : and ' praise ' him for ' ever.

12 All the horns of the ungodly also ' will I ' break : and the horns of the ' righteous shall ' be ex'alted.

PSALM 76

W. TUCKER

135

In Jewry is ' God ' known : his ' Name is ' great in ' Israel.

2 At Salem ' is his ' tabernacle : and his ' dwelling ' in ' Sion.

3 There brake he the ' arrows of the ' bow : the ' shield the ' sword · and the ' battle.

4 Thou art of more ' honour and ' might : than the ' hills ' of the ' robbers.

5 The proud are robbed, they have ' slept their ' sleep : and all the men whose hands were ' mighty have ' found ' nothing.

6 At thy rebuke O ' God of ' Jacob : both the ' chariot and ' horse are ' fallen.

For promotion cometh neither from the east nor from the west: nor yet from the south.

Ps. 75. vs. 7 For promotion cometh neither from the east nor ' from the ' west : nor ' yet ' from the ' south.

121

135   W. TUCKER

7 Thou even thou ' art to be ' feared : and who may stand in thy '
sight when ' thou art ' angry?

8 Thou didst cause thy judgement to be ' heard from ' heaven : the
earth ' trembled ' and was ' still;

9 When God a'rose to ' judgement : and to help ' all the ' meek upon '
earth.

10 The fierceness of man shall ' turn to thy ' praise : and the fierceness
of ' them shalt ' thou re'frain.

11 Promise unto the Lord your God and keep it, all ye that are '
round a'bout him : bring presents unto ' him that ' ought to be '
feared.

12 He shall refrain the ' spirit of ' princes : and is wonderful a-'
mong the ' kings of the ' earth.

PSALM 77

136   J. BATTISHILL

I WILL cry unto God ' with my ' voice : even unto God will I cry with
my voice, and he shall ' hearken ' unto ' me.

2 In the time of my trouble I ' sought the ' Lord : my sore ran and
ceased not in the night-season, my ' soul re'fus-ed ' comfort.

3 When I am in heaviness I will ' think upon ' God : when my heart
is ' vexed I ' will com'plain.

4 Thou holdest mine ' eyes ' waking : I am so feeble ' that I ' cannot '
speak.

5 I have considered the ' days of ' old : and the ' years ' that are ' past.

6 I call to re'membrance my ' song : and in the night I commune with
mine own heart and ' search ' out my ' spirits.

7 Will the Lord absent him'self for ' ever : and will he ' be no ' more in'treated?

8 Is his mercy clean ' gone for ' ever : and is his promise come utterly to an ' end for ' ever'more?

9 Hath God forgotten ' to be ' gracious : and will he shut up his loving'kindness ' in dis'pleasure?

10 And I said, It is mine ' own in'firmity : but I will remember the years of the right hand ' of the ' most ' Highest.

11 I will remember the ' works of the ' Lord : and call to mind thy ' wonders of ' old ' time.

12 I will think also of ' all thy ' works : and my talking shall ' be of ' thy ' doings.

13 Thy way O ' God is ' holy : who is so ' great a ' God as ' our God?

14 Thou art the God that ' doeth ' wonders : and hast declared thy ' power a'mong the ' people.

15 Thou hast mightily de'livered thy ' people : even the ' sons of ' Jacob and ' Joseph.

16 The waters saw thee O God, the waters saw thee and ' were a'fraid : the ' depths ' also were ' troubled.

17 The clouds poured out water the ' air ' thundered : and thine ' arrows ' went a'broad.

18 The voice of thy thunder was heard ' round a'bout : the lightnings shone upon the ground, the earth was ' moved and ' shook with'al.

19 Thy way is in the sea, and thy paths in the ' great ' waters : and thy ' footsteps ' are not ' known.

20 Thou leddest thy ' people like ' sheep : by the ' hand of ' Moses and ' Aaron.

DAY 15 EVENING

PSALM 78

HEAR my law ' O my ' people : incline your ears ' unto the words of my ' mouth.

2 I will open my ' mouth in a ' parable : I will de'clare hard sentences of ' old;

3 Which we have ' heard and ' known : and ' such as our fathers have ' told us;

4 That we should not hide them from the children of the gene-rations to ' come : but to shew the honour of the Lord, his mighty and wonderful ' works that ' he hath ' done.

5 He made a covenant with Jacob, and gave ' Israel a ' law : which he commanded our fore'fathers to ' teach their ' children;

6 That their pos'terity might ' know it : and the children which were ' yet un'born;

7 To the intent that when ' they came ' up : they might ' shew their children the ' same;

8 That they might put their ' trust in ' God : and not to forget the works of God, but to ' keep ' his com'mandments;

9 And not to be as their forefathers, a faithless and stubborn · gene'ration : a generation that set not their heart aright, and whose spirit cleaveth not ' stedfastly ' unto ' God;

10 Like as the ' children of ' Ephraim : who being harnessed and carrying bows, turned themselves ' back in the ' day of ' battle.

11 They kept not the ' covenant of ' God : and ' would not ' walk in his law;

12 But forgat what ' he had ' done : and the wonderful works that he had ' shew-ed ' for them.

13 Marvellous things did he in the sight of our forefathers, in the land of ' Egypt : even ' in the ' field of ' Zoan.

14 He divided the sea and ' let them go ' through : he made the '
waters to ' stand on an ' heap.

15 In the day-time also he led them ' with a ' cloud : and all the night
through ' with a ' light of ' fire.

16 He clave the hard rocks ' in the ' wilderness : and gave them drink
thereof, as it had been ' out of the ' great ' depth.

17 He brought waters out of the ' stony ' rock : so that it ' gush-ed '
out · like the ' rivers.

18 Yet for all this they sin-ned ' more a'gainst him : and provoked the
most ' Highest ' in the ' wilderness.

19 They tempted God ' in their ' hearts : and required ' meat ' for their '
lust.

20 They spake against God ' also ' saying : Shall God prepare a ' table '
in the ' wilderness?

2nd 21 He smote the stony rock indeed, that the waters gushed out and the
Part   streams ' flowed with'al : but can he give bread also, or provide '
flesh for ' his ' people?

22 When the Lord heard this ' he was ' wroth : so the fire was kindled
in Jacob, and there came up heavy dis'pleasure a'gainst ' Israel;

23 Because they believed ' not in ' God : and ' put not their '
trust in his ' help.

24 So he commanded the ' clouds a'bove : and ' opened the ' doors of '
heaven.

25 He rained down manna also upon them ' for to ' eat : and '
gave them ' food from ' heaven.

26 So man did eat ' angels' ' food : for he ' sent them ' meat e'nough.

27 He caused the east-wind to blow ' under ' heaven : and through his
power he brought ' in the ' south-west'wind.

J. GOSS

138

28 He rained flesh upon them as ' thick as ' dust : and feathered fowls '
like as the ' sand of the ' sea.

29 He let it fall a'mong their ' tents : even round a'bout their '
habi'tation.

30 So they did eat and were well filled, for he gave them their '
own de'sire : they were not disap'pointed ' of their ' lust.

31 But while the meat was yet in their mouths, the heavy wrath of
God came upon them, and slew the ' wealthiest ' of them : yea
and smote down the chosen ' men that ' were in ' Israel.

32 But for all this they ' sinned yet ' more : and believed ' not his '
wondrous ' works.

* 33 Therefore their days did ' he con'sume in ' vanity : ' and their '
years in ' trouble.

34 When he slew ' them they ' sought him : and turned them early
and in'quired ' after ' God.

35 And they remembered that ' God was their ' strength : and that the
high ' God was ' their re'deemer.

36 Nevertheless they did but flatter him ' with their ' mouth : and
dissembled ' with him ' in their ' tongue.

37 For their heart was not ' whole with ' him : neither continued they '
stedfast ' in his ' covenant.

Therefore their days did he con - sume in   vanity: and their years   in   trouble.

33 Therefore their days did he con'sume in ' vanity : and their ' years ' in ' trouble.

38 But he was so merciful that he forgave ' their mis'deeds : and de'stroy-ed ' them ' not.

39 Yea many a time turned he his ' wrath a'way : and would not suffer his whole dis'pleasure ' to a'rise.

40 For he considered that they ' were but ' flesh : and that they were even a wind that passeth away and ' cometh ' not a'gain.

41 Many a time did they provoke him ' in the ' wilderness : and ' grieved him ' in the ' desert.

42 They turned back and ' tempted ' God : and moved the ' Holy ' One in ' Israel.

43 They thought not ' of his ' hand : and of the day when he delivered them ' from the ' hand of the ' enemy;

2nd 44 How he had wrought his ' miracles in ' Egypt : and his wonders '
Part   in the ' field of ' Zoan.

45 He turned their waters ' into ' blood : so that they ' might not ' drink of the ' rivers.

46 He sent lice among them and de'voured them ' up : and ' frogs ' to de'stroy them.

47 He gave their fruit ' unto the ' caterpillar : and their ' labour ' unto the ' grasshopper.

48 He destroyed their ' vines with ' hailstones : and their ' mulberry'trees with the ' frost.

49 He smote their cattle ' also with ' hailstones : and their ' flocks with ' hot ' thunder-bolts.

50 He cast upon them the furiousness of his wrath, anger dis-' pleasure and ' trouble : and sent ' evil ' angels a'mong them.

51 He made a way to his indignation, and spared not their ' soul from ' death : but gave their life ' over ' to the ' pestilence;

52 And smote all the ' first-born in ' Egypt : the most principal and mightiest ' in the ' dwellings of ' Ham.

Change to Chant 139 overleaf

127

R. P. GOODENOUGH

139

53 But as for his own people, he led them ' forth like ' sheep : and carried them in the ' wilderness ' like a ' flock.

54 He brought them out safely that they ' should not ' fear : and overwhelmed their ' enemies ' with the ' sea.

55 And brought them within the ' borders · of his ' sanctuary : even to his mountain which he purchased ' with his ' right ' hand.

56 He cast out the heathen ' also be'fore them : caused their land to be divided among them for an heritage, and made the tribes of Israel to ' dwell in ' their ' tents.

57 So they tempted and displeased the ' most high ' God : and kept not ' his ' testimonies;

58 But turned their backs and fell away ' like their ' forefathers : starting aside ' like a ' broken ' bow.

2nd Part 59 For they grieved him with their ' hill'altars : and provoked him to dis'pleasure ' with their ' images.

60 When God heard this ' he was ' wroth : and took ' sore displeasure at ' Israel.

61 So that he forsook the ' tabernacle in ' Silo : even the tent that he had ' pitched a'mong ' men.

62 He delivered their power ' into cap'tivity : and their beauty into the ' enemy's ' hand.

63 He gave his people over also ' unto the ' sword : and was wroth with ' his in'heritance.

64 The fire consumed their ' young ' men : and their maidens were not ' given to ' marriage.

65 Their priests were ' slain with the ' sword : and there were no widows to ' make lamen'tation.

Vss 66-end   J. STAFFORD SMITH

66 So the Lord awaked as one ' out of ' sleep : and like a '
   giant re'freshed with ' wine.

67 He smote his enemies in the ' hinder ' parts : and put them '
   to a per'petual ' shame.

68 He refused the ' tabernacle of ' Joseph : and ' chose not the '
   tribe of ' Ephraim;

69 But chose the ' tribe of ' Judah : even the hill of ' Sion ' which he '
   loved.

70 And there he built his ' temple on ' high : and laid the foundation
   of it, like the ground which ' he hath ' made con'tinually.

71 He chose David ' also his ' servant : and ' took him a'way from the '
   sheep-folds.

72 As he was following the ewes great with ' young ones he '
   took him : that he might feed Jacob his people and ' Israel '
   his in'heritance.

73 So he fed them with a faithful and ' true ' heart : and ruled them '
   prudently with ' all his ' power.

DAY 16   MORNING

PSALM 79

R. COOKE

O God the heathen are come into ' thine in'heritance : thy holy temple
have they defiled, and made Je'rusalem an ' heap of ' stones.

2 The dead bodies of thy servants have they given, to be meat unto
   the ' fowls of the ' air : and the flesh of thy saints ' unto the '
   beasts of the ' land.

R. COOKE

140

3 Their blood have they shed like water on every ' side of Je'rusalem :
and ' there was ' no man to ' bury them.

4 We are become an open shame ' to our ' enemies : a very scorn and
derision unto them ' that are ' round a'bout us.

5 Lord how long wilt ' thou be ' angry : shall thy jealousy ' burn like '
fire for ' ever?

6 Pour out thine indignation upon the heathen that ' have not '
known thee : and upon the kingdoms that have not ' called up-'
on thy ' Name.

7 For they have de'vour-ed ' Jacob : and ' laid ' waste his
dwelling-place.

8 O remember not our old sins, but have mercy upon us ' and that '
soon : for we are ' come to ' great ' misery.

9 Help us O God of our salvation, for the glory ' of thy ' Name : O
deliver us, and be merciful unto our sins ' for thy ' Name's ' sake.

*   10 Wherefore ' do the ' heathen ' say : ' Where is ' now their ' God?

11 O let the vengeance of thy servants' blood ' that is ' shed : be openly
shewed upon the ' heathen ' in our ' sight.

12 O let the sorrowful sighing of the prisoners ' come be'fore thee
according to the greatness of thy power, preserve thou those that
are ap'pointed to ' die.

13 And for the blasphemy wherewith our neighbours have blas-
phem-ed ' thee : reward thou them O Lord ' seven-fold
into their ' bosom.

Wherefore   do   the   heathen   say: where   is   now   their   God?

10 Wherefore do the ' heathen ' say : where is ' now ' their ' God?

14 So we that are thy people and sheep of thy pasture, shall give thee '
thanks for ' ever : and will alway be shewing forth thy praise
from gene'ration to ' gene'ration.

PSALM 80

G. HOLDEN

41

HEAR O thou Shepherd of Israel, thou that leadest Joseph ' like a '
sheep : shew thyself also, thou that ' sittest up'on the ' cherubims.

2 Before Ephraim Benjamin ' and Ma'nasses : stir up thy '
strength and ' come and ' help us.

2nd
Part
3 Turn us a'gain O ' God : shew the light of thy countenance ' and we '
shall be ' whole.

4 O Lord ' God of ' hosts : how long wilt thou be angry ' with thy '
people that ' prayeth?

5 Thou feedest them with the ' bread of ' tears : and givest them '
plenteousness of ' tears to ' drink.

6 Thou hast made us a very strife ' unto our ' neighbours : and our '
enemies ' laugh us to ' scorn.

7 Turn us again thou ' God of ' hosts : shew the light of thy
countenance ' and we ' shall be ' whole.

8 Thou hast brought a vine ' out of ' Egypt : thou hast cast ' out the '
heathen and ' planted it.

9 Thou ' madest ' room for it : and when it had taken ' root it '
filled the ' land.

10 The hills were covered ' with the ' shadow of it : and the boughs
thereof were ' like the ' goodly ' cedar-trees.

11 She stretched out her branches ' unto the ' sea : and her ' boughs '
unto the ' river.

131

G. HOLDE[

141

12 Why hast thou then broken ' down her ' hedge : that all they tha
go ' by pluck ' off her ' grapes?

13 The wild boar out of the wood doth ' root it ' up : and the wild
beasts of the ' field de'vour it.

2nd 14 Turn thee again thou God of hosts, look ' down from ' heaven
Part be'hold and ' visit this ' vine;

15 And the place of the vineyard that thy right ' hand hath ' planted
and the branch that thou ' madest so ' strong for thy'self.

16 It is burnt with fire and ' cut ' down : and they shall perish at the
re'buke of ' thy ' countenance.

17 Let thy hand be upon the man of thy ' right ' hand : and upon the
son of man, whom thou madest so strong ' for thine ' own ' self.

18 And so will not we go ' back from ' thee : O let us live, and we shall
call up'on thy ' Name.

2nd 19 Turn us again O Lord ' God of ' hosts : shew the light of th
Part countenance ' and we ' shall be ' whole.

PSALM 81

Vss 1-11 and Gloria

J. BATTISHILL

142

SING we merrily unto ' God our ' strength : make a cheerful noise
unto the ' God of ' Jacob.

2 Take the psalm bring ' hither the ' tabret : the ' merry
harp with the ' lute.

3 Blow up the trumpet in the ' new ' moon : even in the tim
appointed, and up'on our ' solemn ' feast-day.

4 For this was made a ' statute for ' Israel : and a ' law of the
God of ' Jacob.

5 This he ordained in Joseph ' for a ' testimony : when he came out of the land of Egypt, and had ' heard a ' strange ' language.

6 I eased his shoulder ' from the ' burden : and his hands were ' delivered from ' making the ' pots.

7 Thou calledst upon me in troubles, and ' I de'livered thee : and heard thee what time as the ' storm ' fell up'on thee.

* 8 I ' prov-ed ' thee ' also : ' at the ' waters of ' strife.

9 Hear O my people, and I will assure ' thee O ' Israel : if thou wilt ' hearken ' unto ' me,

10 There shall no strange god ' be in ' thee : neither shalt thou worship ' any ' other ' god.

2nd Part 11 I am the Lord thy God, who brought thee out of the ' land of ' Egypt : open thy mouth ' wide and ' I shall ' fill it.

143

12 But my people would not ' hear my ' voice : and ' Israel ' would not o'bey me.

13 So I gave them up unto their ' own hearts' ' lusts : and let them follow their ' own i'magi'nations.

14 O that my people would have hearkened ' unto ' me : for if ' Israel had ' walked in my ' ways,

8 I proved ' thee ' also : at the ' waters ' of ' strife.

133

15 I should soon have put ' down their ' enemies : and turned my '
hand a'gainst their ' adversaries.

16 The haters of the Lord should have been ' found ' liars : but their
time ' should have en'dured for ' ever.

17 He should have fed them also with the ' finest ' wheat-flour : and
with honey out of the stony rock should ' I have ' satisfied ' thee.

DAY 16   EVENING

PSALM 82

GOD standeth in the congre'gation of ' princes : he is a ' Judge a'mong
gods.

2 How long will ye ' give wrong ' judgement : and accept the ' persons
of the un'godly?

3 Defend the ' poor and ' fatherless : see that such as are in need and
ne'cessity ' have ' right.

4 Deliver the ' outcast and ' poor : save them from the ' hand
of the un'godly.

5 They will not be learned nor understand, but walk on ' still in
darkness : all the foundations of the ' earth are ' out of ' course.

6 I have said ' Ye are ' gods : and ye are all the ' children ' of the most
Highest.

7 But ye shall ' die like ' men : and ' fall like ' one of the ' princes.

8 Arise O God, and judge ' thou the ' earth : for thou shalt take all
heathen to ' thine in'heritance.

PSALM 83

H. BISHOP

45

HOLD not thy tongue O God, keep ' not still ' silence : re-' frain not thy'self O ' God.

2 For lo thine enemies ' make a ' murmuring : and they that hate thee ' have lift ' up their ' head.

3 They have imagined craftily a'gainst thy ' people : and taken ' counsel a'gainst thy ' secret ones.

4 They have said, Come and let us root them out, that they be no ' more a ' people : and that the name of Israel may be no ' more ' in re'membrance.

5 For they have cast their heads together with ' one con'sent : and ' are con'federate a'gainst thee;

6 The tabernacles of the Edomites ' and the ' Ismaelites : the ' Moab'ites and ' Hagarenes;

7 Gebal and ' Ammon and ' Amalek : the Philistines with ' them that ' dwell at ' Tyre.

8 Assur also is ' join-ed ' with them : and have ' holpen the ' children of ' Lot.

9 But do thou to them as ' unto the ' Madianites : unto Sisera and unto Jabin ' at the ' brook of ' Kison;

10 Who ' perished at ' Endor : and be'came · as the ' dung of the ' earth.

11 Make them and their princes like ' Oreb and ' Zeb : yea make all their princes like as ' Zeba ' and Sal'mana;

12 Who say Let us ' take to our'selves : the ' houses of ' God · in pos-' session.

13 O my God make them like ' unto a ' wheel : and as the ' stubble be'fore the ' wind;

14 Like as the fire that burneth ' up the ' wood : and as the ' flame that con'sumeth the ' mountains.

H. BISHOP

145

15 Persecute them even so ' with thy ' tempest : and make them a'fraid ' with thy ' storm.

16 Make their faces a'shamed O ' Lord : that ' they may ' seek thy ' Name.

17 Let them be confounded and vexed ever ' more and ' more : let them be ' put to ' shame and ' perish.

18 And they shall know that thou whose Name ' is Je'hovah : art only the most Highest ' over ' all the ' earth.

PSALM 84

G. J. ELVEY

146

O HOW amiable ' are thy ' dwellings : thou ' Lord ' of ' hosts!

2 My soul hath a desire and longing, to enter into the ' courts of the ' Lord : my heart and my flesh rejoice ' in the ' living ' God.

3 Yea the sparrow hath found her an house, and the swallow a nest where she may ' lay her ' young : even thy altars, O Lord of hosts my ' King and ' my ' God.

4 Blessed are they that ' dwell in thy ' house : they will be ' alway ' praising ' thee.

5 Blessed is the man whose ' strength is in ' thee : in whose ' heart are ' thy ' ways.

6 Who going through the vale of misery, use it ' for a ' well : and the ' pools are ' filled with ' water.

2nd
Part
7 They will go from ' strength to ' strength : and unto the God of gods appeareth every ' one of ' them in ' Sion.

8 O Lord God of hosts ' hear my ' prayer : hearken ' O ' God of Jacob.

9 Behold O God ' our de'fender : and look upon the ' face of ' thine A'nointed.

10 For one day ' in thy ' courts : is ' better ' than a ' thousand.

11 I had rather be a door-keeper in the ' house of my ' God : than to ' dwell in the ' tents of un'godliness.

12 For the Lord God is a ' light and de'fence : the Lord will give grace and worship, and no good thing shall he withhold from them that ' live a ' godly ' life.

13 O Lord ' God of ' hosts : blessed is the man that ' putteth his ' trust in ' thee.

PSALM 85

LORD thou art become gracious ' unto thy ' land : thou hast turned a'way the cap'tivity of ' Jacob.

2 Thou hast forgiven the offence of ' thy ' people : and ' covered ' all their ' sins.

2nd Part 3 Thou hast taken away all ' thy dis'pleasure : and turned thyself from thy ' wrathful ' indig'nation.

4 Turn us then O ' God our ' Saviour : and let thine ' anger ' cease ' from us.

5 Wilt thou be displeased at ' us for ' ever : and wilt thou stretch out thy wrath from one gene'ration ' to an'other?

6 Wilt thou not turn again and ' quicken ' us : that thy people ' may re'joice in ' thee?

7 Shew us thy ' mercy O ' Lord : and ' grant us ' thy sal'vation.

8 I will hearken what the Lord God will ' say con'cerning me : for he shall speak peace unto his people and to his saints, ' that they ' turn not a'gain.

9 For his salvation is nigh ' them that ' fear him : that ' glory may ' dwell in our ' land.

10 Mercy and truth are ' met to'gether : righteousness and ' peace have ' kissed each ' other.

11 Truth shall flourish ' out of the ' earth : and righteousness hath ' look-ed ' down from ' heaven.

F. A. G. OUSELEY

147

12 Yea the Lord shall shew ' loving'kindness : and our ' land shall '
give her ' increase.

13 Righteousness shall ' go be'fore him : and he shall direct his ' going '
in the ' way.

DAY 17   MORNING

PSALM 86

J. TURL

148

Bow down thine ear O ' Lord and ' hear me : for ' I am ' poor and in '
misery.

2 Preserve thou my soul for ' I am ' holy : my God save thy servant
that ' putteth his ' trust in ' thee.

3 Be merciful unto ' me O ' Lord : for I will ' call ' daily up'on thee.

4 Comfort the ' soul of thy ' servant : for unto thee O Lord do ' I lift
up my ' soul.

5 For thou Lord art ' good and ' gracious : and of great mercy unto all
them that ' call up'on thee.

6 Give ear Lord ' unto my ' prayer : and ponder the ' voice of my
humble de'sires.

7 In the time of my trouble I will ' call upon ' thee : for ' thou
hearest ' me.

8 Among the gods there is none like unto ' thee O ' Lord : there is no
one that can ' do as ' thou ' doest.

9 All nations whom thou hast made shall come and worship ' thee O '
Lord : and shall ' glori'fy thy ' Name.

*   10 For thou art great and ' doest ' wondrous ' things : ' thou art '
God a'lone.

11 Teach me thy way O Lord, and I will ' walk in thy ' truth : O knit
my heart unto thee that ' I may ' fear thy ' Name.

12 I will thank thee O Lord my God with ' all my ' heart : and will
praise thy ' Name for ' ever'more.

2nd 13 For great is thy ' mercy ' toward me : and thou hast delivered my
Part soul ' from the ' nethermost ' hell.

14 O God the proud are ' risen a'gainst me : and the congregations
of naughty men have sought after my soul, and have not set '
thee be'fore their ' eyes.

15 But thou O Lord God art full of com'passion and ' mercy : long-
suffering ' plenteous in ' goodness and ' truth.

16 O turn thee then unto me and have ' mercy up'on me : give thy
strength unto thy servant and ' help the ' son of thine ' handmaid.

17 Shew some token upon me for good, that they who hate me may see
it and ' be a'shamed : because thou Lord hast ' holpen ' me and '
comforted me.

Ps. 86 vs. 10 For thou art great and doest ' wondrous ' things : thou ' art ' God a'lone.

PSALM 87

 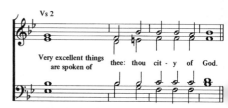

Single Chant

> HER foundations are upon the ' holy ' hills : the Lord loveth the gates of Sion more than ' all the ' dwellings of ' Jacob.

½   2 Very excellent things are spoken of ' thee : thou ' city of ' God.

3 I will think upon ' Rahab and ' Babylon : with ' them that ' know ' me.

4 Behold ye the ' Philistines ' also : and they of Tyre with the Morians, lo ' there was ' he ' born.

5 And of Sion it shall be reported that he was ' born in ' her : and the most ' High shall ' stablish ' her.

6 The Lord shall rehearse it when he writeth ' up the ' people : that ' he was ' born ' there.

7 The singers also and trumpeters shall ' he re'hearse : All my fresh ' springs shall ' be in ' thee.

PSALM 88

> O LORD God of my salvation, I have cried day and ' night be'fore thee O let my prayer enter into thy presence, incline thine ' ear unto my ' calling.

2 For my soul is ' full of ' trouble : and my life draweth ' nigh ' unto hell.

Ps. 87 vs. 2 Very excellent things are ' spoken of ' thee : thou ' city ' of ' God.

3 I am counted as one of them that go down ' into the ' pit : and I have been even as a ' man that ' hath no ' strength.

4 Free among the dead, like unto them that are wounded and ' lie in the ' grave : who are out of remembrance, and are ' cut a-' way from thy ' hand.

5 Thou hast laid me in the ' lowest ' pit : in a place of ' darkness and ' in the ' deep.

6 Thine indignation lieth ' hard up'on me : and thou hast ' vexed me with ' all thy ' storms.

7 Thou hast put away mine acquaintance ' far ' from me : and made me to ' be ab'hor-red ' of them.

8 I am so ' fast in ' prison : that I ' cannot ' get ' forth.

9 My sight faileth for ' very ' trouble : Lord I have called daily upon thee, I have stretched forth my ' hands ' unto ' thee.

10 Dost thou shew wonders a'mong the ' dead : or shall the dead rise ' up a'gain and ' praise thee?

11 Shall thy loving-kindness be shewed ' in the ' grave : or thy ' faithfulness ' in de'struction?

12 Shall thy wondrous works be known ' in the ' dark : and thy righteousness in the land where ' all things ' are for'gotten?

13 Unto thee have I ' cried O ' Lord : and early shall my ' prayer ' come be'fore thee.

14 Lord why abhorrest ' thou my ' soul : and hidest ' thou thy ' face ' from me?

15 I am in misery, and like unto him that is at the ' point to ' die : even from my youth up thy terrors have I suffered ' with a ' troubled ' mind.

16 Thy wrathful displeasure ' goeth ' over me : and the ' fear of thee ' hath un'done me.

17 They came round about me ' daily like ' water : and compassed me to'gether on ' every ' side.

18 My lovers and friends hast thou ' put a'way from me : and hid mine ac'quaintance ' out of my ' sight.

DAY 17 EVENING

PSALM 89

MY song shall be alway of the loving-kindness ' of the ' Lord : with my mouth will I ever be shewing thy truth from one gene'ration ' to an'other.

2 For I have said, Mercy shall be set ' up for ' ever : thy truth shalt thou ' stablish ' in the ' heavens.

3 I have made a covenant ' with my ' chosen : I have sworn ' unto ' David my ' servant;

4 Thy seed will I ' stablish for ' ever : and set up thy throne from one gene'ration ' to an'other.

5 O Lord the very heavens shall praise thy ' wondrous ' works : and thy truth in the congre'gation ' of the ' saints.

6 For who is he a'mong the ' clouds : that shall be com'par-ed ' unto the ' Lord?

7 And what is he a'mong the ' gods : that shall be ' like ' unto the ' Lord?

8 God is very greatly to be feared in the council ' of the ' saints : and to be had in reverence of all ' them that are ' round a'bout him.

9 O Lord God of hosts, who is ' like unto ' thee : thy truth most mighty Lord ' is on ' every ' side.

10 Thou rulest the ' raging · of the ' sea : thou stillest the waves there'of when ' they a'rise.

11 Thou hast subdued Egypt ' and de'stroyed it : thou hast scattered thine enemies abroad ' with thy ' mighty ' arm.

12 The heavens are thine, the earth ' also is ' thine : thou hast laid the foundation of the round world and ' all that ' therein ' is.

13 Thou hast made the ' north and the ' south : Tabor and Hermon shall re'joice in ' thy ' Name.

14 Thou hast a ' mighty ' arm : strong is thy hand and ' high is thy right ' hand.

142

15 Righteousness and equity are the habitation ' of thy ' seat : mercy and truth shall ' go be'fore thy ' face.

16 Blessed is the people O Lord that can re'joice in ' thee : they shall ' walk in the ' light of thy ' countenance.

17 Their delight shall be daily ' in thy ' Name : and in thy righteous-ness ' shall they ' make their ' boast.

18 For thou art the glory ' of their ' strength : and in thy loving-kindness thou ' shalt lift ' up our ' horns.

2nd *Part* 19 For the Lord is ' our de'fence : the Holy One of ' Israel ' is our ' King.

20 Thou spakest sometime in visions unto thy ' saints and ' saidst : I have laid help upon one that is mighty, I have exalted one ' chosen ' out of the ' people.

21 I have found ' David my ' servant : with my holy oil have ' I a'nointed ' him.

22 My hand shall ' hold him ' fast : and my ' arm shall ' strengthen ' him.

23 The enemy shall not be able to ' do him ' violence : the son of ' wickedness ' shall not ' hurt him.

24 I will smite down his foes be'fore his ' face : and ' plague ' them that ' hate him.

25 My truth also and my mercy ' shall be ' with him : and in my Name shall his ' horn ' be ex'alted.

26 I will set his dominion also ' in the ' sea : and his ' right hand ' in the ' floods.

27 He shall call me, Thou ' art my ' Father : my God ' and my ' strong sal'vation.

28 And I will make ' him my ' first-born : higher than the ' kings ' of the ' earth.

29 My mercy will I keep for him for ' ever'more : and my covenant ' shall stand ' fast with ' him.   *V. 30 overleaf 2nd Part*

143

Vss 20-36   J. GOSS

152

2nd   30 His seed also will I make to en'dure for ' ever : and his '
Part   throne as the ' days of ' heaven.

31 But if his children for'sake my ' law : and ' walk not ' in my '
   judgements;

32 If they break my statutes, and keep not ' my com'mandments :
   I will visit their offences with the rod ' and their ' sin with '
   scourges.

33 Nevertheless my loving-kindness will I not utterly ' take '
   from him : nor ' suffer my ' truth to ' fail.

34 My covenant will I not break, nor alter the thing that is gone '
   out of my ' lips : I have sworn once by my holiness, that I '
   will not ' fail ' David.

35 His seed shall en'dure for ' ever : and his seat is ' like as the '
   sun be'fore me.

36 He shall stand fast for evermore ' as the ' moon : and as the '
   faithful ' witness in ' heaven.

Vss 37-50   E. J. HOPKIN

153

37 But thou hast abhorred and forsaken ' thine A'nointed : and '
   art dis'pleased ' at him.

38 Thou hast broken the covenant ' of thy ' servant : and ' cast his
   crown · to the ' ground.

39 Thou hast overthrown ' all his ' hedges : and ' broken ' down his
   strong holds.

40 All they that go ' by ' spoil him : and he is be'come a reproach to his ' neighbours.

41 Thou hast set up the right hand ' of his ' enemies : and made all his
   adversaries ' to re'joice.

42 Thou hast taken away the ' edge of his ' sword : and givest him not '
   victory ' in the ' battle.

43 Thou hast put ' out his ' glory : and cast his ' throne ' down to the '
   ground.

44 The days of his youth ' hast thou ' shortened : and ' covered him '
   with dis'honour.

45 Lord how long wilt thou hide thy'self for ' ever : and shall thy '
   wrath ' burn like ' fire?

46 O remember how ' short my ' time is : wherefore hast thou made '
   all ' men for ' nought?

47 What man is he that liveth and shall ' not see ' death : and shall he
   deliver his soul ' from the ' hand of ' hell?

48 Lord where are thy old ' loving'kindnesses : which thou swarest
   unto ' David ' in thy ' truth?

49 Remember Lord the rebuke that thy ' servants ' have : and how I do
   bear in my bosom the re'bukes of ' many ' people;

50 Wherewith thine enemies have blas'phem-ed ' thee : and slandered
   the ' footsteps of ' thine A'nointed.

154

(return to chant 151 for Gloria)

Unison
2nd Pt. 50a Praised be the Lord for ' ever'more : A'men and ' A'men.

---

50 Wherewith thine enemies have blasphemed thee, and slandered the footsteps of '
   thine A'nointed : Praised be the Lord for evermore ' Amen and ' A'men.

DAY 18 MORNING

PSALM 90

155

Lord thou hast ' been our ' refuge : from one gene'ration ' to an'other.

2 Before the mountains were brought forth, or ever the earth and the '
world were ' made : thou art God from ever'lasting and '
world without ' end.

3 Thou turnest ' man to de'struction : again thou sayest, Come a-'
gain ye ' children of ' men.

4 For a thousand years in thy sight ' are but as ' yesterday : seeing
that is ' past · as a ' watch in the ' night.

5 As soon as thou scatterest them they are ' even as a ' sleep : and
fade away ' suddenly ' like the ' grass.

6 In the morning it is green and ' groweth ' up : but in the evening it
is cut down ' dri-ed ' up and ' withered.

7 For we consume away in ' thy dis'pleasure : and are afraid at thy '
wrathful ' indig'nation.

8 Thou hast set our mis'deeds be'fore thee : and our secret '
sins in the ' light of thy ' countenance.

9 For when thou art angry all our ' days are ' gone : we bring our
years to an end, as it ' were a ' tale that is ' told.

10 The days of our age are threescore years and ten, and though men
be so strong that they come to ' fourscore ' years : yet is their
strength then but labour and sorrow, so soon passeth it a'way and '
we are ' gone.

11 But who regardeth the ' power of thy ' wrath : for even thereafter
as a man feareth ' so is ' thy dis'pleasure.

12 So teach us to ' number our ' days : that we may ap'ply our '
hearts unto ' wisdom.

146

156

13 Turn thee again O Lord ' at the ' last : and be ' gracious ' unto thy '
servants.

14 O satisfy us with thy mercy ' and that ' soon : so shall we rejoice
and be glad ' all the ' days of our ' life.

15 Comfort us again now, after the time that ' thou hast ' plagued us :
and for the years where'in we have ' suffered ad'versity.

16 Shew thy ' servants thy ' work : and their ' children ' thy ' glory.

2nd 17 And the glorious majesty of the Lord our God ' be up'on us : prosper
Part   thou the work of our hands upon us, O ' prosper ' thou our '
handy-work.

PSALM 91

157

WHOSO dwelleth under the defence of the ' most ' High : shall
abide under the ' shadow ' of the Al'mighty.

2 I will say unto the Lord, Thou art my ' hope and my ' strong hold :
my God in ' him will ' I ' trust.

3 For he shall deliver thee from the ' snare · of the ' hunter : and '
from the ' noisome ' pestilence.

4 He shall defend thee under his wings, and thou shalt be safe '
under his ' feathers : his faithfulness and truth shall ' be thy '
shield and ' buckler.

5 Thou shalt not be afraid for any ' terror by ' night : nor for the '
arrow that ' flieth by ' day;

6 For the pestilence that ' walketh in ' darkness : nor for the sickness
that de'stroyeth ' in the ' noon-day.

R. WOODWARD

157

7 A thousand shall fall beside thee, and ten thousand at ' thy right ' hand : but it shall ' not come ' nigh ' thee.

8 Yea with thine eyes shalt ' thou be'hold : and see the re'ward of ' the un'godly.

9 For thou Lord ' art my ' hope : thou hast set thine house of de'fence ' very ' high.

10 There shall no evil happen ' unto ' thee : neither shall any ' plague come ' nigh thy ' dwelling.

11 For he shall give his angels charge ' over ' thee : to ' keep thee in ' all thy ' ways.

12 They shall bear thee ' in their ' hands : that thou hurt not thy ' foot a'gainst a ' stone.

13 Thou shalt go upon the ' lion and ' adder : the young lion and the dragon shalt thou ' tread ' under thy ' feet.

14 Because he hath set his love upon me, therefore will ' I de-' liver him : I will set him up, because ' he hath ' known my ' Name.

15 He shall call upon me and ' I will ' hear him : yea I am with him in trouble, I will de'liver him and ' bring him to ' honour.

16 With long ' life will I ' satisfy him : and ' shew him ' my sal'vation.

PSALM 92

J. NARES

158

It is a good thing to give thanks ' unto the ' Lord : and to sing praises unto thy ' Name ' O most ' Highest;

2 To tell of thy loving-kindness early ' in the ' morning : and of thy ' truth in the ' night'season;

3 Upon an instrument of ten strings, and up'on the ' lute : upon a loud instrument ' and up'on the ' harp.

4 For thou Lord hast made me glad ' through thy ' works : and I will rejoice in giving praise for the ope'rations ' of thy ' hands.

5 O Lord how glorious ' are thy ' works : thy ' thoughts are ' very ' deep.

6 An unwise man doth not well con'sider ' this : and a fool ' doth not ' under'stand it.

7 When the ungodly are green as the grass, and when all the workers of ' wickedness do ' flourish : then shall they be destroyed for ever, but thou Lord art the most ' Highest for ' ever'more.

8 For lo thine enemies O Lord, lo thine ' enemies shall ' perish : and all the workers of ' wickedness shall ' be de'stroyed.

9 But mine horn shall be exalted like the ' horn of an ' unicorn : for I am a'nointed with ' fresh ' oil.

10 Mine eye also shall see his ' lust of mine ' enemies : and mine ear shall hear his desire of the wicked that a'rise ' up a'gainst me.

11 The righteous shall flourish ' like a ' palm-tree : and shall spread abroad ' like a ' cedar in ' Libanus.

12 Such as are planted in the ' house of the ' Lord : shall flourish in the ' courts of the ' house of our ' God.

13 They also shall bring forth more ' fruit in their ' age : and shall be ' fat and ' well'liking.

14 That they may shew how true the Lord my ' strength ' is : and that there is ' no un'righteousness in ' him.

DAY 18   EVENING
PSALM 93

E. G. MONK

159

THE Lord is King, and hath put on ' glorious ap'parel : the Lord hath put on his apparel and ' girded him'self with ' strength.

2 He hath made the round ' world so ' sure : that it ' cannot ' be ' moved.

3 Ever since the world began hath thy seat ' been pre'pared : thou ' art from ' ever'lasting.

E. G. MONK

159

4 The floods are risen O Lord, the floods have lift ' up their ' voice :
the ' floods lift ' up their ' waves.

5 The waves of the sea are mighty and ' rage ' horribly : but yet the
Lord who ' dwelleth on ' high is ' mightier.

6 Thy testimonies O Lord are ' very ' sure : holiness be'cometh thine '
house for ' ever.

PSALM 94

S. ELVEY

160

O LORD God to whom ' vengeance be'longeth : thou God to whom
vengeance be'longeth ' shew thy ' self.

2 Arise thou ' Judge of the ' world : and reward the proud ' after '
their de'serving.

3 Lord how long ' shall the un'godly : how long ' shall the un'godly '
triumph?

4 How long shall all wicked doers speak ' so dis'dainfully : and
make such ' proud ' boasting?

5 They smite down thy ' people O ' Lord : and ' trouble ' thine
heritage.

6 They murder the ' widow · and the ' stranger : and ' put the
fatherless to ' death.

7 And yet they say, Tush the ' Lord shall not ' see : neither shall the
God of ' Jacob re'gard it.

8 Take heed ye unwise a'mong the ' people : O ye fools ' when will ye
under'stand?

9 He that planted the ear shall ' he not ' hear : or he that made the '
eye shall ' he not ' see?

10 Or he that ' ' nurtureth the ' heathen : it is he that teacheth man
knowledge, ' shall not ' he ' punish?

2nd Pt. 11 The Lord knoweth the ' thoughts of ' man : that ' they ' are but '
vain.

12 Blessed is the man whom thou ' chastenest O ' Lord : and '
teachest him ' in thy ' law;

13 That thou mayest give him patience in ' time of ad'versity : until
the pit be digged ' up for ' the un'godly.

14 For the Lord will not ' fail his ' people : neither will he for'sake '
his in'heritance;

15 Until righteousness turn again ' unto ' judgement : all such as are '
true in ' heart shall ' follow it.

16 Who will rise up with me a'gainst the ' wicked : or who will take
my part a'gainst the ' evil'doers?

17 If the Lord ' had not ' helped me : it had not failed but my '
soul had been ' put to ' silence.

18 But when I said My ' foot hath ' slipt : thy mercy O ' Lord ' held me '
up.

19 In the multitude of the sorrows that I had ' in my ' heart : thy
comforts ' have re'fresh-ed my ' soul.

20 Wilt thou have any thing to do with the ' stool of ' wickedness :
which imagineth ' mischief ' as a ' law?

21 They gather them together against the ' soul of the ' righteous :
and con'demn the ' innocent ' blood.

22 But the Lord ' is my ' refuge : and my ' God is the ' strength of my '
confidence.

23 He shall recompense them their wickedness, and destroy them in
their ' own ' malice : yea the ' Lord our ' God shall de'stroy them.

DAY 19   MORNING
PSALM 95

W. CROTCH

161

f   O COME let us ' sing unto the ' Lord : let us heartily rejoice in the '
strength of ' our sal'vation.

2 Let us come before his ' presence with ' thanksgiving : and shew
ourselves ' glad in ' him with ' psalms.

3 For the Lord is a ' great ' God : and a great ' King above ' all ' gods.

4 In his hand are all the ' corners · of the ' earth : and the strength of
the ' hills is ' his ' also.

2nd   5 The sea is his and ' he ' made it : and his hands pre'pared the ' dry '
Part   land.

p   6 O come let us worship and ' fall ' down : and kneel be'fore the '
Lord our ' Maker.

7 For he is the ' Lord our ' God : and we are the people of his pasture,
and the ' sheep of ' his ' hand.

mf 8 To-day if ye will hear his voice, harden ' not your ' hearts : as in the
provocation, and as in the day of temp'tation ' in the ' wilderness;

*   9 When your ' fathers ' tempted ' me : ' proved me and ' saw my '
works.

10 Forty years long was I grieved with this gene'ration and ' said : It
is a people that do err in their hearts, for they ' have not '
known my ' ways;

11 Unto whom I ' sware · in my ' wrath : that they should not ' enter '
into my ' rest.

When your fa - thers   tempted   me: proved me and saw my works.

Ps. 95 vs. 9 When your fathers ' tempted ' me : proved ' me and ' saw my ' works.

PSALM 96

W. RUSSELL

162

O SING unto the Lord a ' new ' song : sing unto the Lord ' all the ' whole ' earth.

2 Sing unto the Lord and ' praise his ' Name : be telling of his sal'vation from ' day to ' day.

3 Declare his honour ' unto the ' heathen : and his wonders ' unto ' all ' people.

4 For the Lord is great, and cannot ' worthily be ' praised : he is more to be ' feared than ' all ' gods.

5 As for all the gods of the heathen, they ' are but ' idols : but it is the ' Lord that ' made the ' heavens.

6 Glory and worship ' are be'fore him : power and ' honour are ' in his ' sanctuary.

7 Ascribe unto the Lord O ye ' kindreds of the ' people : ascribe unto the ' Lord ' worship and ' power.

8 Ascribe unto the Lord the honour due ' unto his ' Name : bring presents and ' come ' into his ' courts.

9 O worship the Lord in the ' beauty of ' holiness : let the ' whole earth ' stand in ' awe of him.

10 Tell it out among the heathen that the ' Lord is ' King : and that it is he who hath made the round world so fast that it cannot be moved, and how that he shall ' judge the ' people ' righteously.

11 Let the heavens rejoice and let the ' earth be ' glad : let the sea make a noise and ' all that ' therein ' is.

12 Let the field be joyful and ' all that is ' in it : then shall all the trees of the wood re'joice be'fore the ' Lord.

2nd 13 For he cometh, for he cometh to ' judge the ' earth : and with
Part   righteousness to judge the world, and the ' people ' with his ' truth.

PSALM 97

163

THE Lord is King, the earth may be ' glad there'of : yea the multitude of the isles ' may be ' glad there'of.

2 Clouds and darkness are ' round a'bout him : righteousness and judgement are the habi'tation ' of his ' seat.

3 There shall go a ' fire be'fore him : and burn up his ' enemies on ' every ' side.

4 His lightnings gave shine ' unto the ' world : the earth ' saw it and ' was a'fraid.

5 The hills melted like wax at the ' presence of the ' Lord : at the presence of the ' Lord of the ' whole ' earth.

6 The heavens have de'clared his ' righteousness : and all the ' people have ' seen his ' glory.

7 Confounded be all they that worship carved images, and that delight in ' vain ' gods : worship ' him ' all ye ' gods.

8 Sion heard of it ' and re'joiced : and the daughters of Judah were glad be'cause of thy ' judgements O ' Lord.

9 For thou Lord art higher than all that are ' in the ' earth : thou art exalted ' far above ' all ' gods.

10 O ye that love the Lord, see that ye hate the ' thing which is ' evil : the Lord preserveth the souls of his saints, he shall deliver them ' from the ' hand of the un'godly.

11 There is sprung up a ' light for the ' righteous : and joyful gladness for ' such as are ' true'hearted.

12 Rejoice in the ' Lord ye ' righteous : and give thanks for a re'membrance ' of his ' holiness.

DAY 19 EVENING

PSALM 98

G. J. ELVEY

164

O SING unto the Lord a ' new ' song : for he hath ' done ' marvellous ' things.

2 With his own right hand and with his ' holy ' arm : hath he ' gotten him'self the ' victory.

3 The Lord declared ' his sal'vation : his righteousness hath he openly ' shewed in the ' sight of the ' heathen.

4 He hath remembered his mercy and truth, toward the ' house of ' Israel : and all the ends of the world have seen the sal'vation of ' our ' God.

5 Shew yourselves joyful unto the Lord ' all ye ' lands : sing re-' joice and ' give ' thanks.

6 Praise the Lord up'on the ' harp : sing to the ' harp with a ' psalm of ' thanksgiving.

7 With trumpets ' also and ' shawms : O shew yourselves joyful be'fore the ' Lord the ' King.

8 Let the sea make a noise, and all that ' therein ' is : the round world and ' they that ' dwell there'in.

9 Let the floods clap their hands, and let the hills be joyful together be'fore the ' Lord : for he is ' come to ' judge the ' earth.

10 With righteousness shall he ' judge the ' world : and the ' people ' with ' equity.

PSALM 99

165　J. BATTISHILL

Verses 5 and 9 unison

THE Lord is King, be the people never ' so un'patient : he sitteth between the cherubims, be the earth ' never ' so un'quiet.

2 The Lord is ' great in ' Sion : and ' high a'bove all ' people.

3 They shall give thanks ' unto thy ' Name : which is great ' wonder'ful and ' holy.

4 The King's power loveth judgement, thou hast pre'par-ed ' equity : thou hast executed ' judgement and ' righteousness in ' Jacob.

Unison
2nd Pt. 5 O magnify the ' Lord our ' God : and fall down before his ' footstool for ' he is ' holy.

6 Moses and Aaron among his priests, and Samuel among such as call up'on his ' Name : these called upon the ' Lord and ' he ' heard them.

7 He spake unto them out of the ' cloudy ' pillar : for they kept his testimonies, and the ' law that ' he ' gave them.

8 Thou heardest them O ' Lord our ' God : thou forgavest them O God, and ' punishedst their ' own in'ventions.

Unison 9 O magnify the Lord our God, and worship him upon his ' holy ' hill : for the ' Lord our ' God is ' holy.

PSALM 100

166　SAVAGE

O BE joyful in the Lord ' all ye ' lands : serve the Lord with gladness and come before his ' presence ' with a ' song.

2 Be ye sure that the Lord ' he is ' God : it is he that hath made us and not we ourselves, we are his ' people · and the ' sheep of his ' pasture.

3 O go your way into his gates with thanksgiving, and into his ' courts with ' praise : be thankful unto him and ' speak good ' of his ' Name.

4 For the Lord is gracious, his mercy is ' ever'lasting : and his truth endureth from gene'ration to ' gene'ration.

PSALM 101

S. H. NICHOLSON

167

MY song shall be of ' mercy and ' judgement : unto thee O Lord ' will I ' sing.

2 O let me have ' under'standing : in the ' way of ' godliness.

3 When wilt thou come ' unto ' me : I will walk in my house with a ' perfect ' heart.

4 I will take no wicked thing in hand, I hate the ' sins of un'faithfulness : there shall no such cleave ' unto ' me.

5 A froward heart shall de'part from ' me : I will not know a ' wicked ' person.

6 Whoso privily ' slandereth his ' neighbour : him will ' I de'stroy.

7 Whoso hath also a proud look and ' high ' stomach : I will not ' suffer ' him.

8 Mine eyes look upon such as are faithful ' in the ' land : that they may ' dwell with ' me.

9 Whoso leadeth a ' godly ' life : he shall ' be my ' servant.

10 There shall no deceitful person ' dwell in my ' house : he that telleth lies shall not tarry ' in my ' sight.

2nd Part 11 I shall soon destroy all the ungodly that are ' in the ' land : that I may root out all wicked doers from the city ' of the ' Lord.

Glory be to the Father, and ' to the ' Son : and to the ' Holy ' Ghost.

As it was in the beginning, is now and ' ever ' shall be : world without end. ' A'men.   *Alternative chant overleaf*

PSALM 101

F. A. G. OUSELEY

168

My song shall be of ' mercy and ' judgement : unto ' thee O '
Lord will I ' sing.

* 2 O ' let me have ' under'standing : ' in the ' way of ' godliness.

3 When wilt thou come ' unto ' me : I will walk in my house ' with a '
perfect ' heart.

4 I will take no wicked thing in hand, I hate the '
sins of un'faithfulness : there shall ' no such ' cleave unto ' me.

5 A froward heart shall de'part ' from me : I will not ' know a ' wicked '
person.

* 6 Whoso ' privily ' slandereth his ' neighbour : ' him will ' I de'stroy.

7 Whoso hath also a proud look and ' high ' stomach : I ' will not '
suffer ' him.

8 Mine eyes look upon such as are faithful ' in the ' land : that '
they may ' dwell with ' me.

Ps. 101 vs. 2 O let me have ' under'standing : in the ' way of ' godli'ness.
        6 Whoso privily ' slandereth his ' neighbour : him ' — will ' I de'stroy.

* 9 Whoso ' leadeth a ' godly ' life : ' he shall ' be my ' servant.

10 There shall no deceitful person ' dwell in my ' house : he that telleth lies shall not ' tarry ' in my ' sight.

2nd 11 I shall soon destroy all the ungodly that are ' in the ' land : that
Part   I may root out all wicked doers from the ' city ' of the ' Lord.

DAY 20   MORNING

PSALM 102

HEAR my ' prayer O ' Lord : and let my ' crying ' come unto ' thee.

2 Hide not thy face from me in the ' time of my ' trouble : incline thine ear unto me when I call, O ' hear me and ' that right ' soon.

3 For my days are consumed a'way like ' smoke : and my bones are burnt up ' as it ' were a ' fire-brand.

4 My heart is smitten down and ' withered like ' grass : so that I for'get to ' eat my ' bread.

5 For the ' voice of my ' groaning : my bones will scarce ' cleave ' to my ' flesh.

6 I am become like a pelican ' in the ' wilderness : and like an owl ' that is ' in the ' desert.

7 I have watched, and am even as it ' were a ' sparrow : that sitteth a'lone up'on the ' house-top.

8 Mine enemies revile me ' all the day ' long : and they that are mad upon me are ' sworn to'gether a'gainst me.

9 For I have eaten ashes ' as it were ' bread : and ' mingled my ' drink with ' weeping;

10 And that because of thine indig'nation and ' wrath : for thou hast taken me ' up and ' cast me ' down.

nd Pt. 11 My days are ' gone · like a ' shadow : and ' I am ' withered like '
grass.   *Change to Chant 170 overleaf*

Ps. 101 vs. 9 Whoso leadeth a ' godly ' life : he ' shall be ' my ' servant.

12 But thou O Lord shalt en'dure for'ever : and thy remembrance '
    throughout ' all gene'rations.

13 Thou shalt arise and have ' mercy upon ' Sion : for it is time that
    thou have mercy upon her ' yea the ' time is ' come.

2nd 14 And why? thy servants think up'on her ' stones : and it pitieth
Part   them to ' see her ' in the ' dust.

15 The heathen shall fear thy ' Name O ' Lord : and all the '
    kings of the ' earth thy ' majesty;

16 When the Lord shall ' build up ' Sion : and when his ' glory '
    shall ap'pear;

17 When he turneth him unto the prayer of the ' poor ' destitute : and
    des'piseth not ' their de'sire.

18 This shall be written for ' those that come ' after : and the people
    which shall be ' born shall ' praise the ' Lord.

19 For he hath looked ' down from his ' sanctuary : out of the heaven
    did the ' Lord be'hold the ' earth;

20 That he might hear the mournings of such as are ' in cap'tivity :
    and deliver the children ap'pointed ' unto ' death;

21 That they may declare the Name of the ' Lord in ' Sion : and his '
    worship ' at Je'rusalem;

22 When the people are ' gathered to'gether : and the kingdoms '
    also to ' serve the ' Lord.

23 He brought down my strength ' in my ' journey : and ' shortened
    my ' days.

24 But I said, O my God take me not away in the ' midst of mine ' age
    as for thy years they endure ' throughout ' all gene'rations.

25 Thou Lord in the beginning hast laid the foundation ' of the ' earth :
and the ' heavens are the ' work of thy ' hands.

26 They shall perish but ' thou shalt en'dure : they all shall wax '
old as ' doth a ' garment;

27 And as a vesture shalt thou change them, and they ' shall be '
changed : but thou art the same and thy ' years ' shall not ' fail.

28 The children of thy servants ' shall con'tinue : and their seed shall
stand ' fast in ' thy ' sight.   *Return to chant 170 for Gloria*

PSALM 103

PRAISE the Lord ' O my ' soul : and all that is within me ' praise his '
holy ' Name.

2 Praise the Lord ' O my ' soul : and for'get not ' all his ' benefits;

3 Who forgiveth ' all thy ' sin : and ' healeth ' all thine in'firmities;

4 Who saveth thy ' life from de'struction : and crowneth thee with '
mercy and ' loving ' kindness;

5 Who satisfieth thy mouth with ' good ' things : making thee young
and ' lusty ' as an ' eagle.

6 The Lord executeth ' righteousness and ' judgement : for all '
them that are op'pressed with ' wrong.

7 He shewed his ways ' unto ' Moses : his works ' unto the '
children of ' Israel.

8 The Lord is full of com'passion and ' mercy : long-suffering ' and of '
great ' goodness.

9 He will not ' alway be ' chiding : neither ' keepeth he his ' anger for '
ever.

10 He hath not dealt with us ' after our ' sins : nor rewarded us
ac'cording ' to our ' wickednesses.

S. WESLEY

171

11 For look how high the heaven is, in comparison ' of the ' earth : so great is his mercy also ' toward ' them that ' fear him.

12 Look how wide also the east is ' from the ' west : so far hath he ' set our ' sins ' from us.

13 Yea like as a father pitieth his ' own ' children : even so is the Lord merciful ' unto ' them that ' fear him.

14 For he knoweth whereof ' we are ' made : he re'membereth that ' we are but ' dust.

15 The days of man ' are but as ' grass : for he flourisheth ' as a ' flower of the ' field.

16 For as soon as the wind goeth over it ' it is ' gone : and the ' place thereof shall ' know it no ' more.

17 But the merciful goodness of the Lord endureth for ever and ever, upon ' them that ' fear him : and his righteousness up'on ' children's ' children;

18 Even upon such as ' keep his ' covenant : and think upon ' his com'mandments to ' do them.

19 The Lord hath prepared his ' seat in ' heaven : and his kingdom ' ruleth ' over ' all.

20 O praise the Lord ye angels of his, ye that ex'cel in ' strength : ye that fulfil his commandment, and hearken ' unto the ' voice of his ' words.

21 O praise the Lord all ' ye his ' hosts : ye servants of ' his that ' do his ' pleasure.

22 O speak good of the Lord all ye works of his, in all places of ' his do'minion : praise thou the ' Lord ' O my ' soul.

DAY 20 EVENING
PSALM 104

PRAISE the Lord ' O my ' soul : O Lord my God thou art become exceeding glorious, thou art ' clothed with ' majesty and ' honour.

2 Thou deckest thyself with light as it ' were with a ' garment : and spreadest out the ' heavens ' like a ' curtain.

3 Who layeth the beams of his chambers ' in the ' waters : and maketh the clouds his chariot, and walketh up'on the ' wings of the ' wind.

4 He maketh his ' angels ' spirits : and his ' ministers a ' flaming ' fire.

5 He laid the foundations ' of the ' earth : that it never should ' move at ' any ' time.

6 Thou coveredst it with the deep, like as ' with a ' garment : the ' waters ' stand in the ' hills.

7 At thy re'buke they ' flee : at the voice of thy ' thunder ' they are a'fraid.

8 They go up as high as the hills, and down to the ' valleys be'neath : even unto the place which ' thou hast ap'pointed ' for them.

9 Thou hast set them their bounds which they ' shall not ' pass : neither turn a'gain to ' cover the ' earth.

10 He sendeth the springs ' into the ' rivers : which ' run a'mong the ' hills.

11 All beasts of the field ' drink there'of : and the wild ' asses ' quench their ' thirst.

12 Beside them shall the fowls of the air have their ' habi'tation : and ' sing a'mong the ' branches.

13 He watereth the hills ' from a'bove : the earth is ' filled with the ' fruit of thy ' works.

14 He bringeth forth ' grass for the ' cattle : and green ' herb for the ' service of ' men;

163

H. SMAR

172

or

(alternative Chant)   W. MARS

173

15 That he may bring food out of the earth, and wine that maketh gla
the ' heart of ' man : and oil to make him a cheerful countenance
and ' bread to ' strengthen man's ' heart.

16 The trees of the Lord also are ' full of ' sap : even the cedars of
Libanus which ' he hath ' planted;

17 Wherein the birds ' make their ' nests : and the fir-trees are a
dwelling ' for the ' stork.

18 The high hills are a refuge ' for the wild ' goats : and so are the
stony ' rocks for the ' conies.

19 He appointed the moon for ' certain ' seasons : and the sun
knoweth his ' going ' down.

20 Thou makest darkness that it ' may be ' night : wherein all the
beasts of the ' forest do ' move.

21 The lions roaring ' after their ' prey : do ' seek their ' meat from
God.

22 The sun ariseth, and they get them a'way to'gether : and ' lay them
down in their ' dens.

2nd Pt.

*   23 Man goeth ' forth to his ' work and ' to his ' labour : un'til the
evening.

Vs 23

Man goeth forth to his work and to his la - bour: un - til the evening.

Vs 23

Man goeth forth to his work and to his la - bour: un - til the evening.

23 Man goeth forth to his work and ' to his ' labour : un'til the ' eve'ning.

24 O Lord how manifold ' are thy ' works : in wisdom hast thou made
them all, the ' earth is ' full of thy ' riches.

25 So is the great and ' wide sea ' also : wherein are things creeping
innumerable, both ' small and ' great ' beasts.

26 There go the ships, and there is ' that Le'viathan : whom thou hast
made to ' take his ' pastime there'in.

27 These wait ' all upon ' thee : that thou mayest give them ' meat in '
due ' season.

28 When thou givest it ' them they ' gather it : and when thou openest
thy hand ' they are ' filled with ' good.

29 When thou hidest thy face ' they are ' troubled : when thou takest
away their breath they die, and are ' turned a'gain to their ' dust.

30 When thou lettest thy breath go forth they ' shall be ' made : and
thou shalt re'new the ' face of the ' earth.

31 The glorious majesty of the Lord shall en'dure for ' ever : the '
Lord shall re'joice in his ' works.

32 The earth shall ' tremble · at the ' look of him : if he do but '
touch the ' hills · they shall ' smoke.

33 I will sing unto the Lord as ' long as I ' live : I will praise my God '
while I ' have my ' being.

34 And so shall my ' words ' please him : my ' joy shall ' be in the '
Lord.

35 As for sinners, they shall be consumed ' out of the ' earth : and the
un'godly shall ' come to an ' end.

*2nd Pt.*35a Praise ' thou the ' Lord : O my ' soul ' praise the ' Lord.

---

35 As for sinners they shall be consumed out of the earth, and the ungodly shall '
come to an ' end : praise thou the Lord O my ' soul ' praise the ' Lord.

DAY 21   MORNING
PSALM 105

O GIVE thanks unto the Lord, and call up'on his ' name : tell the ' people what ' things he hath ' done.

2 O let your songs be of ' him and ' praise him : and let your talking be of ' all his ' wondrous ' works.

3 Rejoice in his ' holy ' Name : let the heart of them re'joice that ' seek the ' Lord.

4 Seek the ' Lord and his ' strength : seek his ' face ' ever'more.

5 Remember the marvellous works that ' he hath ' done : his wonders and the ' judgements ' of his ' mouth.

6 O ye seed of ' Abraham his ' servant : ye ' children of ' Jacob his ' chosen.

7 He is the ' Lord our ' God : his judgements ' are in ' all the ' world.

8 He hath been alway mindful of his ' covenant and ' promise : that he made to a ' thousand ' gene'rations;

9 Even the covenant that he ' made with ' Abraham : and the ' oath that he ' sware unto ' Isaac;

10 And appointed the same unto ' Jacob for a ' law : and to Israel for an ' ever'lasting ' testament;

11 Saying Unto thee will I give the ' land of ' Canaan : the ' lot of ' your in'heritance;

12 When there were ' yet but a ' few of them : and they ' strangers ' in the ' land;

13 What time as they went from one nation ' to an'other : from one kingdom ' to an'other ' people;

14 He suffered no man to ' do them ' wrong : but reproved even ' kings for ' their ' sakes;

2nd Pt. 15 Touch not ' mine A'nointed : and ' do my ' prophets no ' harm.

16 Moreover he called for a dearth up'on the ' land : and destroyed ' all the pro'vision of ' bread.

166

17 But he had sent a ' man be'fore them : even Joseph who was ' sold to ' be a ' bond-servant;

18 Whose feet they ' hurt in the ' stocks : the iron ' entered ' into his ' soul;

19 Until the time came that his ' cause was ' known : the ' word of the ' Lord ' tried him.

20 The king ' sent and de'livered him : the prince of the ' people ' let him go ' free.

21 He made him lord also ' of his ' house : and ' ruler of ' all his ' substance;

2nd Part 22 That he might inform his princes ' after his ' will : and ' teach his ' senators ' wisdom.

23 Israel also came ' into ' Egypt : and Jacob was a stranger ' in the ' land of ' Ham.

24 And he increased his ' people ex'ceedingly : and made them ' stronger ' than their ' enemies;

2nd Part 25 Whose heart turned, so that they ' hated his ' people : and dealt un'truly ' with his ' servants.

26 Then sent he ' Moses his ' servant : and ' Aaron whom ' he had ' chosen.

27 And these shewed his ' tokens a'mong them : and wonders ' in the ' land of ' Ham.

28 He sent darkness ' and it was ' dark : and they were not o'bedient ' unto his ' word.

29 He turned their waters ' into ' blood : and ' slew ' their ' fish.

30 Their land ' brought forth ' frogs : yea even ' in their ' kings' ' chambers.

31 He spake the word, and there came all ' manner of ' flies : and ' lice in ' all their ' quarters.

32 He gave them ' hail-stones for ' rain : and ' flames of ' fire in their ' land.

33 He smote their vines ' also and ' fig-trees : and destroyed the ' trees that were ' in their ' coasts.

34 He spake the word and the grass-hoppers came, and cater-' pillars in'numerable : and did eat up all the grass in their land, and de'voured the ' fruit of their ' ground.

35 He smote all the first-born ' in their ' land : even the ' chief of ' all their ' strength.

K. J. PYE

174

36 He brought them forth also with ' silver and ' gold : there was not one feeble ' person a'mong their ' tribes.

37 Egypt was glad at ' their de'parting : for they ' were a'fraid of ' them.

38 He spread out a cloud to ' be a ' covering : and fire to give light ' in the ' night'season.

39 At their desire he ' brought ' quails : and he filled them ' with the ' bread of ' heaven.

40 He opened the rock of stone, and the waters ' flow-ed ' out : so that rivers ' ran in the ' dry ' places.

41 For why? he remembered his ' holy ' promise : and ' Abra'ham his ' servant.

42 And he brought forth his ' people with ' joy : and his ' chosen ' with ' gladness;

43 And gave them the ' lands of the ' heathen : and they took the labours of the ' people ' in pos'session;

2nd Pt. 44 That they might ' keep his ' statutes : and ob'serve ' his ' laws.

DAY 21   EVENING

PSALM 106

T. JACKSON

175

O GIVE thanks unto the Lord for ' he is ' gracious : and his ' mercy en'dureth for ' ever.

2 Who can express the noble ' acts of the ' Lord : or ' shew forth all his ' praise?

* 3 Blessed ' are ' they that ' alway keep ' judgement : ' and do ' righteousness.

4 Remember me O Lord, according to the favour that thou bearest ' unto thy ' people : O ' visit me with ' thy sal'vation;

5 That I may see the felicity ' of thy ' chosen : and rejoice in the gladness of thy people, and give ' thanks with ' thine in'heritance.

6 We have sinned ' with our ' fathers : we have done a'miss and ' dealt ' wickedly.

7 Our fathers regarded not thy wonders in Egypt, neither kept they thy great goodness ' in re'membrance : but were disobedient at the sea, even ' at the ' Red ' sea.

8 Nevertheless he helped them for his ' Name's ' sake : that he might make his ' power ' to be ' known.

9 He rebuked the Red sea also, and it was ' dried ' up : so he led them through the ' deep as ' through a ' wilderness.

10 And he saved them from the ' adversaries' ' hand : and delivered them ' from the ' hand of the ' enemy.

11 As for those that troubled them, the waters ' over'whelmed them : there ' was not ' one of them ' left.

12 Then believed ' they his ' words : and sang ' praise ' unto ' him.

13 But within a while they for'gat his ' works : and would ' not a-' bide his ' counsel.

14 But lust came upon them ' in the ' wilderness : and they ' tempted ' God · in the ' desert.

15 And he gave them ' their de'sire : and sent leanness with'al ' into their ' soul.

16 They angered Moses also ' in the ' tents : and ' Aaron the ' saint of the ' Lord.

17 So the earth opened and ' swallowed up ' Dathan : and covered the congre'gation ' of A'biram.

3 Blessed are they that ' alway keep ' judgement : and ' do ' righteous'ness.

T. JACKSON

175

18 And the fire was kindled ' in their ' company : the ' flame burnt '
up the un'godly.

19 They made a ' calf in ' Horeb : and ' worshipped the ' molten '
image.

20 Thus they ' turned their ' glory : into the similitude of a ' calf that '
eateth ' hay.

21 And they forgat ' God their ' Saviour : who had done so ' great '
things in ' Egypt;

22 Wondrous works in the ' land of ' Ham : and fearful things ' by the '
Red ' sea.

2nd   23 So he said he would have destroyed them, had not Moses his chosen
Part   stood before him ' in the ' gap : to turn away his wrathful
indignation ' lest he ' should de'stroy them.

24 Yea they thought scorn of that ' pleasant ' land : and gave no '
credence ' unto his ' word;

25 But murmured ' in their ' tents : and hearkened not ' unto the '
voice of the ' Lord.

26 Then lift he up his ' hand a'gainst them : to over'throw them '
in the ' wilderness;

27 To cast out their seed a'mong the ' nations : and to ' scatter them '
in the ' lands.

28 They joined themselves unto ' Baal'peor : and ate the ' offerings '
of the ' dead.

29 Thus they provoked him to anger with their ' own in'ventions : and
the ' plague was ' great a'mong them.

30 Then stood up ' Phinees and ' prayed : and ' so the ' plague ' ceased.

31 And that was counted unto ' him for ' righteousness : among all
pos'terities for ' ever'more.

32 They angered him also at the ' waters of ' strife : so that he punished '
Moses for ' their ' sakes;

33 Because they pro'voked his ' spirit : so that he spake unad'visedly ' with his ' lips.

34 Neither destroyed ' they the ' heathen : as the ' Lord com'manded ' them;

35 But were mingled a'mong the ' heathen : and ' learn-ed ' their ' works.

36 Insomuch that they worshipped their idols, which turned to their ' own de'cay : yea they offered their sons and their ' daughters ' unto ' devils;

37 And shed innocent blood, even the blood of their sons and ' of their ' daughters : whom they offered unto the idols of Canaan, and the ' land was de'filed with ' blood.

2nd   38 Thus were they stained with their ' own ' works : and went a
Part   whoring ' with their ' own in'ventions.

39 Therefore was the wrath of the Lord kindled a'gainst his ' people : insomuch that he ab'horred his ' own in'heritance.

40 And he gave them over into the ' hands of the ' heathen : and they that ' hated them were ' lords ' over them.

41 Their ' enemies op'pressed them : and ' had them ' in sub'jection.

42 Many a time did ' he de'liver them : but they rebelled against him with their own inventions, and were brought ' down in ' their ' wickedness.

43 Nevertheless, when he saw ' their ad'versity : he ' heard ' their com'plaint.

44 He thought upon his covenant and pitied them, according unto the multitude ' of his ' mercies : yea he made all those that led them away ' captive to ' pity ' them.

45 Deliver us O Lord our God, and gather us from a'mong the ' heathen : that we may give thanks unto thy holy Name, and ' make our ' boast of thy ' praise.

46 Blessed be the Lord God of Israel from everlasting and ' world without ' end : and let all the ' people ' say A'men.

DAY 22 MORNING

PSALM 107

Vss 1-7; 10-14; 17-20; 23-30; 33-end.
W. TURNER

176

Vss 8, 9; 15, 16; 21, 22; 31, 32.
T. ATTWOOD

177

or

177a

(the above chant in the original key.)
T. ATTWOOD

O GIVE thanks unto the Lord for ' he is ' gracious : and his mercy en'dureth for ' ever.

2 Let them give thanks whom the ' Lord hath re'deemed : and delivered ' from the ' hand of the ' enemy;

2nd Part 3 And gathered them out of the lands, from the east and ' from the west : from the ' north and ' from the ' south.

4 They went astray in the wilderness ' out of the ' way : and found no ' city to ' dwell in;

5 Hungry ' and ' thirsty : their ' soul ' fainted in ' them.

p 6 So they cried unto the Lord ' in their ' trouble : and he delivered them ' from ' their dis'tress.

7 He led them forth by the ' right ' way : that they might go to the city ' where they ' dwelt.

f   8 O that men would therefore praise the ' Lord for his ' goodness :
and declare the wonders that he ' doeth for the ' children of ' men!

9 For he satisfieth the ' empty ' soul : and filleth the ' hungry '
soul with ' goodness.

10 Such as sit in darkness, and in the ' shadow of ' death : being fast '
bound in ' misery and ' iron;

11 Because they rebelled against the ' words of the ' Lord : and lightly
regarded the counsel ' of the ' most ' Highest;

2nd 12 He also brought down their ' heart through ' heaviness : they fell
Part   down and ' there was ' none to ' help them.

p   13 So when they cried unto the Lord ' in their ' trouble : he delivered
them ' out of ' their dis'tress.

14 For he brought them out of darkness, and out of the ' shadow of '
death : and ' brake their ' bonds in ' sunder.

f   15 O that men would therefore praise the ' Lord for his ' goodness :
and declare the wonders that he ' doeth for the ' children of ' men!

16 For he hath broken the ' gates of ' brass : and smitten the ' bars of '
iron in ' sunder.

17 Foolish men are plagued for ' their of 'fence : and be'cause of ' their '
wickedness.

18 Their soul abhorred all ' manner of ' meat : and they were even '
hard at ' death's ' door.

p   19 So when they cried unto the Lord ' in their ' trouble : he delivered
them ' out of ' their dis'tress.

20 He sent his ' word and ' healed them : and they were ' saved from '
their de'struction.

f   21 O that men would therefore praise the ' Lord for his ' goodness :
and declare the wonders that he ' doeth for the ' children of ' men!

22 That they would offer unto him the ' sacrifice of ' thanksgiving :
and tell ' out his ' works with ' gladness!

23 They that go down to the ' sea in ' ships : and occupy their '
business in ' great ' waters;

24 These men see the ' works of the ' Lord : and his ' wonders ' in the '
deep.

25 For at his word the stormy ' wind a'riseth : which lifteth ' up the '
waves there'of.

Vss 1-7; 10-14; 17-20; 23-30; 33-end.

W. TURNER

176

Vss 8, 9; 15, 16; 21, 22; 31, 32.

T. ATTWOOD

177

or

(the above chant in the original key.)

T. ATTWOOD

177a

26 They are carried up to the heaven, and down a'gain to the ' deep
their soul melteth a'way be'cause of the ' trouble.

27 They reel to and fro, and stagger like a ' drunken ' man : and are
at their ' wits' ' end.

p   28 So when they cry unto the Lord ' in their ' trouble : he delivereth
them ' out of ' their dis'tress.

29 For he maketh the ' storm to ' cease : so that the ' waves thereof are ' still.

30 Then are they glad, because they ' are at ' rest : and so he bringeth
them unto the ' haven where ' they would ' be.

f   31 O that men would therefore praise the ' Lord for his ' goodness
and declare the wonders that he ' doeth for the ' children of ' men

32 That they would exalt him also in the congre'gation of the ' people
and praise him ' in the ' seat of the ' elders!

33 Who turneth the floods ' into a ' wilderness : and ' drieth ' up the ' water-springs.

34 A fruitful land ' maketh he ' barren : for the wickedness of ' them that ' dwell there'in.

35 Again he maketh the wilderness a ' standing ' water : and water-springs ' of a ' dry ' ground.

36 And there he ' setteth the ' hungry : that they may ' build them a ' city to ' dwell in;

37 That they may sow their land and ' plant ' vineyards : to ' yield them ' fruits of ' increase.

38 He blesseth them, so that they ' multiply ex'ceedingly : and suffereth not their ' cattle ' to de'crease.

39 And again, when they are minished and ' brought ' low : through oppression through ' any ' plague or ' trouble;

40 Though he suffer them to be evil in'treated through ' tyrants : and let them wander out of the ' way ' in the ' wilderness;

2nd 41 Yet helpeth he the poor ' out of ' misery : and maketh him house-
Part   holds ' like a ' flock of ' sheep.

42 The righteous will consider this ' and re'joice : and the mouth of all ' wickedness ' shall be ' stopped.

43 Whoso is wise will ' ponder these ' things : and they shall understand the loving'kindness ' of the ' Lord.

DAY 22   EVENING

PSALM 108

O GOD, my heart is ready my ' heart is ' ready : I will sing and give praise with the best ' member ' that I ' have.

2 Awake thou ' lute and ' harp : I myself ' will a'wake right ' early.

3 I will give thanks unto thee O Lord a'mong the ' people : I will sing praises unto ' thee a'mong the ' nations.

175

4 For thy mercy is greater ' than the ' heavens : and thy truth ' reacheth ' unto the ' clouds.

5 Set up thyself O God a'bove the ' heavens : and thy glory a'bove ' all the ' earth.

6 That thy beloved may ' be de'livered : let thy right hand save ' them and ' hear thou ' me.

7 God hath spoken ' in his ' holiness : I will rejoice therefore and divide Sichem, and mete ' out the ' valley of ' Succoth.

8 Gilead is mine and Ma'nasses is ' mine : Ephraim also is the ' strength of ' my ' head.

2nd Part 9 Judah is my law-giver, Moab ' is my ' wash-pot : over Edom will I cast out my shoe, upon Phi'listia ' will I ' triumph.

10 Who will lead me into the ' strong ' city : and who will ' bring me into ' Edom?

11 Hast not thou forsaken ' us O ' God : and wilt not thou O ' God go forth with our ' hosts?

12 O help us a'gainst the ' enemy : for ' vain is the ' help of ' man.

13 Through God we shall ' do great ' acts : and it is he that shall tread ' down our ' enemies.

PSALM 109

180

HOLD not thy tongue O ' God of my ' praise : for the mouth of the
ungodly, yea the mouth of the de'ceitful is ' opened up'on me.

2 And they have spoken against me with ' false ' tongues : they
compassed me about also with words of hatred, and fought
a'gainst me with'out a ' cause.

3 For the love that I had unto them, lo they take now my ' contrary '
part : but I ' give myself ' unto ' prayer.

4 Thus have they rewarded me ' evil for ' good : and ' hatred for '
my good ' will.

[5 Set thou an ungodly man to be ' ruler ' over him : and let Satan '
stand at ' his right ' hand.

6 When sentence is given upon him, let him ' be con'demned : and let
his ' prayer be ' turned into ' sin.

7 Let his ' days be ' few : and let an'other ' take his ' office.

8 Let his ' children be ' fatherless : and ' his ' wife a ' widow.

9 Let his children be vagabonds and ' beg their ' bread : let them seek
it also ' out of ' desolate ' places.

10 Let the extortioner consume ' all that he ' hath : and let the '
stranger ' spoil his ' labour.

11 Let there be ' no man to ' pity him : nor to have compassion up-'
on his ' fatherless ' children.

12 Let his posterity ' be de'stroyed : and in the next generation let his '
name be ' clean put ' out.

13 Let the wickedness of his fathers be had in remembrance in the '
sight of the ' Lord : and let not the sin of his ' mother be '
done a'way.

14 Let them alway be be'fore the ' Lord : that he may root out the
memorial of ' them from ' off the ' earth.

180

15 And that, because his mind was ' not to do ' good : but persecuted
the poor helpless man, that he might slay him that was ' vex-ed '
at the ' heart.

16 His delight was in cursing, and it shall happen ' unto ' him : he
loved not blessing, therefore shall ' it be ' far ' from him.

17 He clothed himself with cursing, like as ' with a ' raiment : and it
shall come into his bowels like water, and like ' oil ' into his '
bones.

18 Let it be unto him as the cloke that he ' hath up'on him : and as the
girdle that he is ' alway ' girded with'al.

2nd   19 Let it thus happen from the Lord ' unto mine ' enemies : and to
Part   those that speak ' evil a'gainst my ' soul.]

181

20 But deal thou with me O Lord God, according ' unto thy ' Name :
for ' sweet ' is thy ' mercy.

21 O deliver me for I am ' helpless and ' poor : and my ' heart is '
wounded with'in me.

22 I go hence like the shadow ' that de'parteth : and am driven a'way '
as the ' grasshopper.

23 My knees are ' weak through ' fasting : my flesh is dried ' up for '
want of ' fatness.

24 I became also a reproach ' unto ' them : they that looked up'on me '
shaked their ' heads.

25 Help me O ' Lord my ' God : O save me ac'cording ' to thy ' mercy.

26 And they shall know how that this is ' thy ' hand : and that ' thou '
Lord hast ' done it.

27 Though they curse yet ' bless ' thou : and let them be confounded
that rise up against me, but ' let thy ' servant re'joice.

2nd 28 Let mine adversaries be ' clothed with ' shame : and let them cover
Part themselves with their own con'fusion ' as with a ' cloke.

29 As for me, I will give great thanks unto the Lord ' with my ' mouth :
and ' praise him a'mong the ' multitude.

30 For he shall stand at the right ' hand of the ' poor : to save his soul '
from un'righteous ' judges.

DAY 23   MORNING

PSALM 110

P. HENLEY

182

THE Lord said unto ' my ' Lord : Sit thou on my right hand until I '
make thine ' enemies thy ' footstool.

2 The Lord shall send the rod of thy power ' out of ' Sion : be thou
ruler, even in the ' midst a'mong thine ' enemies.

3 In the day of thy power shall the people offer thee free-will offerings,
with an ' holy ' worship : the dew of thy birth is ' of the '
womb of the ' morning.

4 The Lord sware and will ' not re'pent : Thou art a priest for ever
after the ' order ' of Mel'chisedech.

5 The Lord upon ' thy right ' hand : shall wound even ' kings in the '
day of his ' wrath.

6 He shall judge among the heathen, he shall fill the places with the '
dead ' bodies : and smite in sunder the heads ' over ' divers '
countries.

2nd 7 He shall drink of the ' brook in the ' way : therefore ' shall he · lift '
Part up his ' head.

179

PSALM 111

E. J. HOPKINS

183

I WILL give thanks unto the Lord with my ' whole ' heart : secretly among the faithful and ' in the ' congre'gation.

2 The works of the ' Lord are ' great : sought out of all ' them that have ' pleasure there'in.

3 His work is worthy to be praised and ' had in ' honour : and his ' righteousness en'dureth for ' ever.

4 The merciful and gracious Lord hath so done his ' marvellous ' works : that they ' ought to be ' had in re'membrance.

5 He hath given meat unto ' them that ' fear him : he shall ever be ' mindful ' of his ' covenant.

6 He hath shewed his people the ' power of his ' works : that he may give them the ' heritage ' of the ' heathen.

7 The works of his hands are ' verity and ' judgement : all ' his com'mandments are ' true.

8 They stand fast for ' ever and ' ever : and are ' done in ' truth and ' equity.

9 He sent redemption ' unto his ' people : he hath commanded his covenant for ever, holy and ' reverend ' is his ' Name.

10 The fear of the Lord is the be'ginning of ' wisdom : a good understanding have all they that do thereafter, the ' praise of it en'dureth for ' ever.

PSALM 112

W. FITZHERBERT

184

BLESSED is the man that ' feareth the ' Lord : he hath great de'light in ' his com'mandments.

2 His seed shall be ' mighty upon ' earth : the generation of the ' faithful ' shall be ' blessed.

3 Riches and plenteousness shall be ' in his ' house : and his ' righteousness en'dureth for ' ever.

4 Unto the godly there ariseth up ' light in the ' darkness : he is ' merciful ' loving and ' righteous.

5 A good man is ' merciful and ' lendeth : and will ' guide his ' words with dis'cretion.

6 For he shall ' never be ' moved : and the righteous shall be had in ' ever'lasting re'membrance.

7 He will not be afraid of any ' evil ' tidings : for his heart standeth fast and be'lieveth ' in the ' Lord.

8 His heart is established and ' will not ' shrink : until he see his de'sire up'on his ' enemies.

9 He hath dispersed abroad and given ' to the ' poor : and his ' righteousness remaineth for ever, his horn shall ' be ex'alted with ' honour.

10 The ungodly shall see it and ' it shall ' grieve him : he shall gnash with his teeth and consume away, the de'sire of the un'godly shall ' perish.

PSALM 113

F. A. G. OUSELEY

185

PRAISE the ' Lord ye ' servants : O ' praise the ' Name of the ' Lord.

2 Blessed be the ' Name of the ' Lord : from this time ' forth for ' ever'more.

3 The Lord's ' Name is ' praised : from the rising up of the sun unto the ' going ' down of the ' same.

4 The Lord is high a'bove all ' heathen : and his ' glory a'bove the ' heavens.

5 Who is like unto the Lord our God, that hath his ' dwelling so ' high : and yet humbleth himself to behold the things that ' are in ' heaven and ' earth?

6 He taketh up the simple ' out of the ' dust : and lifteth the ' poor '
out of the ' mire;

7 That he may set him ' with the ' princes : even with the ' princes '
of his ' people.

8 He maketh the barren woman to ' keep ' house : and to be a ' joyful '
mother of ' children.

DAY 23   EVENING

PSALM 114

WHEN Israel came ' out of ' Egypt : and the house of Jacob from
a'mong the ' strange ' people,

2 Judah ' was his ' sanctuary : and ' Israel ' his do'minion.

3 The sea saw ' that and ' fled : Jordan ' was ' driven ' back.

4 The mountains ' skipped like ' rams : and the little ' hills like '
young ' sheep.

5 What aileth thee O thou sea ' that thou ' fleddest : and thou Jordan
that ' thou wast ' driven ' back?

6 Ye mountains that ye ' skipped like ' rams : and ye little ' hills like '
young ' sheep?

7 Tremble thou earth at the presence ' of the ' Lord : at the presence '
of the ' God of ' Jacob;

8 Who turned the hard rock into a ' standing ' water : and the flint-
stone ' into a ' springing ' well.

PSALM 115

187

NOT unto us O Lord, not unto us, but unto thy Name ' give the '
praise : for thy loving mercy and for thy ' truth's ' sake.

2 Wherefore shall the ' heathen ' say : Where is ' now their ' God?

3 As for our God ' he is in ' heaven : he hath done whatsoever '
pleas-ed ' him.

4 Their idols are ' silver and ' gold : even the work of ' men's ' hands.

5 They have ' mouths and ' speak not : eyes have ' they and ' see not.

6 They have ' ears and ' hear not : noses have ' they and ' smell not.

7 They have hands and handle not, feet have ' they and ' walk not :
neither speak they ' through their ' throat.

8 They that make them are ' like unto ' them : and so are all such as
put their ' trust in ' them.

188

9 But thou house of Israel ' trust thou · in the ' Lord : he is their '
succour ' and de'fence.

10 Ye house of Aaron, put your ' trust in the ' Lord : he is their '
helper · and de'fender.

11 Ye that fear the Lord, put your ' trust in the ' Lord : he is their '
helper · and de'fender.

12 The Lord hath been mindful of us and ' he shall ' bless us : even he
shall bless the house of Israel, he shall bless the ' house of ' Aaron.

13 He shall bless them that ' fear the ' Lord : both ' small and ' great.

14 The Lord shall increase you ' more and ' more : you ' and your '
children.

15 Ye are the blessed ' of the ' Lord : who made ' heaven and ' earth.

188

16 All the whole heavens ' are the ' Lord's : the earth hath he given to the ' children of ' men.

17 The dead praise not ' thee O ' Lord : neither all they that go ' down into ' silence.

18 But we will ' praise the ' Lord : from this time forth for evermore. ' Praise the ' Lord.

Glory be to the Father, and ' to the ' Son : and to the ' Holy ' Ghost.

As it was in the beginning, is now and ' ever ' shall be : world without end. ' A'men.

or   PSALM 115

189

Not unto us O Lord, not unto us, but unto thy Name ' give the ' praise : for thy loving mercy and ' for thy ' truth's ' sake.

*   2 Wherefore ' shall the ' heathen ' say : ' Where is ' now their ' God?

3 As for our God ' he is in ' heaven : he hath done whatso'ever ' pleas-ed ' him.

4 Their idols are ' silver and ' gold : even the ' work of ' men's ' hands.

*   5 They have ' mouths and ' speak ' not : ' eyes have ' they and ' see not.

*   6 They have ' ears and ' hear ' not : ' noses have ' they and ' smell not.

7 They have hands and handle not, feet have ' they and ' walk not : neither ' speak they ' through their ' throat.

Ps. 115 vs. 2 Wherefore shall the ' heathen ' say : Where is ' now ' their ' God?

8 They that make them are ' like unto ' them : and so are all such as ' put their ' trust in ' them.

190

9 But thou house of Israel ' trust thou · in the ' Lord : he is their ' succour ' and de'fence.

10 Ye house of Aaron, put your ' trust · in the ' Lord : he is their ' helper ' and de'fender.

11 Ye that fear the Lord, put your ' trust · in the ' Lord : he is their ' helper ' and de'fender.

12 The Lord hath been mindful of us and ' he shall ' bless us : even he shall bless the house of Israel, he shall ' bless the ' house of ' Aaron.

13 He shall bless them that ' fear the ' Lord : both ' small ' and ' great.

*   14 The Lord shall in'crease you ' more and ' more : ' you and ' your ' children.

5 They have ' mouths and ' speak not : eyes ' have ' they and ' see not.
6 They have ' ears and ' hear not : noses ' have ' they and ' smell not.
14 The Lord shall increase you ' more and ' more : you ' and ' your ' children.

15 Ye are the ' blessed of the ' Lord : who ' made ' heaven and ' earth.

16 All the whole heavens ' are the ' Lord's : the earth hath he ' given to the ' children of ' men.

17 The dead praise not ' thee O ' Lord : neither all they that go ' down ' into ' silence.

18 But we will ' praise the ' Lord : from this time forth for evermore. ' Praise ' – the ' Lord.

DAY 24   MORNING

PSALM 116

I AM ' well ' pleased : that the Lord hath ' heard the ' voice of my ' prayer;

2 That he hath inclined his ear ' unto ' me : therefore will I call upon ' him as ' long as I ' live.

3 The snares of death compassed me ' round a'bout : and the pains of ' hell gat ' hold up'on me.

4 I shall find trouble and heaviness, and I will call upon the ' Name of the ' Lord : O Lord I be'seech thee de'liver my ' soul.

5 Gracious is the ' Lord and ' righteous : yea ' our ' God is ' merciful.

6 The Lord pre'serveth the ' simple : I was in ' misery ' and he ' helped me.

7 Turn again then unto thy rest ' O my ' soul : for the ' Lord ' hath re'warded thee.

8 And why? thou hast delivered my ' soul from ' death : mine eyes from tears ' and my ' feet from ' falling.

9 I will walk be'fore the ' Lord : in the ' land ' of the ' living.

10 I believed and therefore will I speak, but I was ' sore ' troubled : I said in my haste, ' All ' men are ' liars.

11 What reward shall I give ' unto the ' Lord : for all the benefits that ' he hath ' done unto ' me?

12 I will receive the ' cup of sal'vation : and call up'on the ' Name of the ' Lord.

13 I will pay my vows now in the presence of ' all his ' people : right dear in the sight of the ' Lord · is the ' death of his ' saints.

14 Behold O Lord how that ' I am thy ' servant : I am thy servant and the son of thine handmaid, thou hast ' broken my ' bonds in ' sunder.

15 I will offer to thee the ' sacrifice of ' thanksgiving : and will call up'on the ' Name of the ' Lord.

16 I will pay my vows unto the Lord, in the sight of ' all his ' people : in the courts of the Lord's house, even in the midst of thee O Jerusalem. ' Praise ' – the ' Lord.

PSALM 117

192

O PRAISE the Lord ' all ye ' heathen : praise ' him ' all ye ' nations.

2 For his merciful kindness is ever more and more ' towards ' us : and the truth of the Lord endureth for ever. ' Praise ' – the ' Lord.

PSALM 118

193

O GIVE thanks unto the Lord for ' he is ' gracious : because his '
mercy en'dureth for ' ever.

2 Let Israel now confess that ' he is ' gracious : and that his '
mercy en'dureth for ' ever.

3 Let the house of Aaron ' now con'fess : that his ' mercy en-'
dureth for ' ever.

4 Yea let them now that fear the ' Lord con'fess : that his '
mercy en'dureth for ' ever.

194

5 I called upon the ' Lord in ' trouble : and the Lord ' heard ' me at
large.

6 The Lord is ' on my ' side : I will not ' fear what ' man doeth
unto me.

7 The Lord taketh my part with ' them that ' help me : therefore
shall I see my de'sire up'on mine ' enemies.

8 It is better to ' trust in the ' Lord : than to ' put · any ' confidence in
man.

9 It is better to ' trust in the ' Lord : than to ' put · any ' confidence in
princes.

10 All nations compassed me ' round a'bout : but in the Name of the
Lord will ' I de'stroy them.

11 They kept me in on every side, they kept me in I say on ' every
side : but in the Name of the ' Lord will ' I de'stroy them.

12 They came about me like bees, and are extinct even as the fire
a'mong the ' thorns : for in the Name of the ' Lord I ' will destroy them.

Vss 13-18   J. ALCOCK

195

13 Thou hast thrust sore at me that ' I might ' fall : but the ' Lord was ' my ' help.

14 The Lord is my ' strength and my ' song : and is be'come ' my sal'vation.

15 The voice of joy and health is in the dwellings ' of the ' righteous : the right hand of the Lord bringeth ' mighty ' things to ' pass.

16 The right hand of the Lord ' hath the pre'eminence : the right hand of the Lord bringeth ' mighty ' things to ' pass.

17 I shall not ' die but ' live : and de'clare the ' works of the ' Lord.

18 The Lord hath chastened and cor'rected ' me : but he hath not given me ' over ' unto ' death.

Vss 19-end   E. G. MONK

196

19 Open me the ' gates of ' righteousness : that I may go into them and give ' thanks ' unto the ' Lord.

20 This is the ' gate of the ' Lord : the ' righteous shall ' enter ' into it.

21 I will thank thee for ' thou hast ' heard me : and art be'come ' my sal'vation.

22 The same stone which the ' builders re'fused : is become the ' headstone ' in the ' corner.

2nd Pt. 23 This is the ' Lord's ' doing : and it is ' marvellous ' in our ' eyes.

24 This is the day which the ' Lord hath ' made : we will re-' joice and be ' glad in ' it.

25 Help me ' now O ' Lord : O Lord ' send us ' now pros'perity.

26 Blessed be he that cometh in the ' Name of the ' Lord : we have wished you good luck, ye that ' are of the ' house of the ' Lord.

27 God is the Lord who hath ' shewed us ' light : bind the sacrifice with cords, yea even ' unto the ' horns of the ' altar.

28 Thou art my God and ' I will ' thank thee : thou art my ' God and ' I will ' praise thee.

29 O give thanks unto the Lord for ' he is ' gracious : and his ' mercy en'dureth for ' ever.

DAY 24   EVENING

PSALM 119

BLESSED are those that are undefiled ' in the ' way : and ' walk in the ' law of the ' Lord.

2 Blessed are they that ' keep his ' testimonies : and seek him ' with their ' whole ' heart.

3 For they who ' do no ' wickedness : walk ' in ' his ' ways.

4 Thou ' hast ' charged : that we shall ' diligently ' keep thy com-' mandments.

5 O that my ways were made ' so di'rect : that ' I might ' keep thy ' statutes!

6 So shall I not ' be con'founded : while I have re'spect unto ' all thy com'mandments.

7 I will thank thee with an un'feign-ed ' heart : when I shall have learned the ' judgements ' of thy ' righteousness.

8 I will ' keep thy ' ceremonies : O for'sake me ' not ' utterly.

WHEREWITHAL shall a young man ' cleanse his ' way : even by ruling him'self ' after thy ' word.

10 With my whole heart ' have I ' sought thee : O let me not go wrong ' out of ' thy com'mandments.

11 Thy words have I hid with'in my ' heart : that I ' should not ' sin a'gainst thee.

12 Blessed art ' thou O ' Lord : O ' teach me ' thy ' statutes.

13 With my lips have ' I been ' telling : of all the ' judgements ' of thy ' mouth.

14 I have had as great delight in the ' way of thy ' testimonies : as in ' all ' manner of ' riches.

15 I will talk of ' thy com'mandments : and have re'spect ' unto thy ' ways.

16 My delight shall be ' in thy ' statutes : and I will ' not for'get thy ' word.

Vss 17 - 32   G. HEATHCOTE

98

O DO well ' unto thy ' servant : that I may ' live and ' keep thy ' word.

18 Open ' thou mine ' eyes : that I may see the ' wondrous ' things of thy ' law.

19 I am a stranger up'on ' earth : O hide not ' thy com'mandments ' from me.

20 My soul breaketh out for the very ' fervent de'sire : that it hath ' alway ' unto thy ' judgements.

21 Thou hast re'buked the ' proud : and cursed are they that do ' err from ' thy com'mandments.

198

22 O turn from me ' shame and re'buke : for ' I have ' kept thy ' testimonies.

23 Princes also did sit and ' speak a'gainst me : but thy servant is ' occupied ' in thy ' statutes.

* 24 For ' thy ' testimonies ' are my de'light : and ' my ' counsellors.

———————

MY soul cleaveth ' to the ' dust : O quicken thou me ac'cording ' to thy ' word.

26 I have acknowledged my ways ' and thou ' heardest me : O ' teach me ' thy ' statutes.

27 Make me to understand the way of ' thy com'mandments : and so shall I ' talk of thy ' wondrous ' works.

28 My soul melteth away for ' very ' heaviness : comfort thou me ac'cording ' unto thy ' word.

29 Take from me the ' way of ' lying : and cause thou me to make ' much of ' thy ' law.

30 I have chosen the ' way of ' truth : and thy judgements ' have I ' laid be'fore me.

31 I have stuck ' unto thy ' testimonies : O ' Lord con'found me ' not.

32 I will run the way of ' thy com'mandments : when thou hast ' set my ' heart at ' liberty.

24 For thy testimonies are ' my de'light : and ' my ' – ' counsellors.

DAY 25 MORNING

TEACH me O Lord the ' way of thy ' statutes : and I shall ' keep it ' unto the ' end.

34 Give me understanding and I shall ' keep thy ' law : yea I shall keep it ' with my ' whole ' heart.

35 Make me to go in the path of ' thy com'mandments : for there'in is ' my de'sire.

* 36 In'cline my ' heart ' unto thy ' testimonies : and ' not to ' covetousness.

37 O turn away mine eyes, lest they be'hold ' vanity : and quicken thou ' me in ' thy ' way.

38 O stablish thy word ' in thy ' servant : that ' I may ' fear ' thee.

39 Take away the rebuke that ' I am a'fraid of : for thy ' judgements ' are ' good.

40 Behold my delight is in ' thy com'mandments : O ' quicken me ' in thy ' righteousness.

———————

LET thy loving mercy come also unto ' me O ' Lord : even thy salvation ac'cording ' unto thy ' word.

42 So shall I make answer unto ' my blas'phemers : for my ' trust is ' in thy ' word.

43 O take not the word of thy truth utterly ' out of my ' mouth : for my ' hope is ' in thy ' judgements.

In - cline my heart unto thy test - i - mo - nies: and not to covetousness.

36 Incline my heart ' unto thy ' testimonies : and ' not to ' covetous'ness.

J. JONES

199

*   44 So shall I ' alway ' keep thy ' law : ' yea for ' ever and ' ever.

     45 And I will ' walk at ' liberty : for I ' seek ' thy com'mandments.

     46 I will speak of thy testimonies also, even be'fore ' kings : and ' will not ' be a'shamed.

*   47 And my de'light shall ' be in ' thy com'mandments : ' which I have ' loved.

     48 My hands also will I lift up unto thy commandments ' which I have ' loved : and my ' study · shall ' be in thy ' statutes.

S. ELVEY

200

     O THINK upon thy servant as con'cerning thy ' word : wherein thou hast caused ' me to ' put my ' trust.

     50 The same is my comfort ' in my ' trouble : for thy ' word hath quickened ' me.

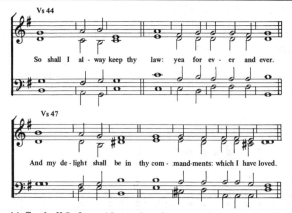

44 So shall I alway ' keep thy ' law : yea for ' ever ' and ' ever.
47 And my delight shall be in ' thy com'mandments : which ' I ' have ' loved.

51 The proud have had me exceedingly ' in de'rision : yet have I not ' shrink-ed ' from thy ' law.

* 52 For I remembered thine ever'lasting ' judgements O ' Lord : ' and re'ceiv-ed ' comfort.

53 I am ' horribly a'fraid : for the ungodly ' that for'sake thy ' law.

54 Thy statutes have ' been my ' songs : in the ' house ' of my ' pilgrimage.

55 I have thought upon thy Name O Lord in the ' night'season : and have ' kept ' thy ' law.

56 This ' I ' had : be'cause I ' kept thy com'mandments.

THOU art my ' portion O ' Lord : I have ' promised to ' keep thy ' law.

58 I made my humble petition in thy presence with my ' whole ' heart : O be merciful unto me ac'cording ' to thy ' word.

59 I called mine own ' ways to re'membrance : and turned my ' feet ' unto thy ' testimonies.

60 I made haste and prolonged ' not the ' time : to ' keep ' thy com'mandments.

61 The congregations of the un'godly have ' robbed me : but I have ' not for'gotten thy ' law.

62 At midnight I will rise to give ' thanks unto ' thee : be'cause of thy ' righteous ' judgements.

63 I am a companion of all ' them that ' fear thee : and ' keep ' thy com'mandments.

64 The earth O Lord is ' full of thy ' mercy : O ' teach me ' thy ' statutes.

52 For I remembered thine everlasting ' judgements O ' Lord : and ' – re'ceived ' comfort.

O LORD thou hast dealt graciously ' with thy ' servant : ac'cording '
unto thy ' word.

66 O learn me true under'standing and ' knowledge : for I have be-'
liev-ed ' thy com'mandments.

67 Before I was troubled ' I went ' wrong : but ' now · have I ' kept thy '
word.

68 Thou art ' good and ' gracious : O ' teach me ' thy ' statutes.

69 The proud have imagined a ' lie a'gainst me : but I will keep thy
commandments ' with my ' whole ' heart.

70 Their heart is as ' fat as ' brawn : but my delight hath ' been in '
thy ' law.

71 It is good for me that I have ' been in ' trouble : that ' I may '
learn thy ' statutes.

72 The law of thy mouth is dearer ' unto ' me : than ' thousands of '
gold and ' silver.

DAY 25   EVENING

THY hands have ' made me and ' fashioned me : O give me understanding, that I may ' learn ' thy com'mandments.

74 They that fear thee will be glad ' when they ' see me : because I
have ' put my ' trust in thy ' word.

75 I know O Lord that thy ' judgements are ' right : and that thou of very faithfulness hast ' caused me ' to be ' troubled.

76 O let thy merciful kindness ' be my ' comfort : according to thy ' word ' unto thy ' servant.

77 O let thy loving mercies come unto me that ' I may ' live : for thy ' law is ' my de'light.

78 Let the proud be confounded, for they go wickedly about ' to de-' stroy me : but I will be ' occupied in ' thy com'mandments.

79 Let such as fear thee and have ' known thy ' testimonies : be ' turn-ed ' unto ' me.

80 O let my heart be sound ' in thy ' statutes : that ' I be ' not a-' shamed.

————————

MY soul hath longed for ' thy sal'vation : and I have a good ' hope be'cause of thy ' word.

82 Mine eyes long sore ' for thy ' word : saying ' O when ' wilt thou ' comfort me?

83 For I am become like a bottle ' in the ' smoke : yet do I ' not for-' get thy ' statutes.

84 How many are the ' days of thy ' servant : when wilt thou be ' avenged of ' them that ' persecute me?

85 The proud have ' dig-ged ' pits for me : which ' are not ' after thy ' law.

86 All thy com'mandments are ' true : they persecute me falsely ' O be ' thou my ' help.

87 They had almost made an end of me up'on ' earth : but I for-' sook not ' thy com'mandments.

88 O quicken me after thy ' loving'kindness : and so shall I keep the ' testimonies ' of thy ' mouth.

Vss 89 - 104   W. CROTCH

202

O LORD ' thy ' word : en'dureth for ' ever in ' heaven.

90 Thy truth also remaineth from one generation ' to an'other : thou hast laid the foundation of the ' earth and ' it a'bideth.

Vss 89 - 104

W. CROTCH

202

91 They continue this day according ' to thine ' ordinance : for ' all things ' serve ' thee.

92 If my delight had not been ' in thy ' law : I should have ' perished ' in my ' trouble.

93 I will never forget ' thy com'mandments : for with them ' thou hast ' quickened ' me.

94 I am ' thine O ' save me : for I have ' sought ' thy com'mandments.

95 The ungodly laid wait for me ' to de'stroy me : but ' I will con-' sider thy ' testimonies.

96 I see that all things ' come to an ' end : but thy commandment ' is ex'ceeding ' broad.

LORD what love have I ' unto thy ' law : all the day long ' is my ' study ' in it.

98 Thou through thy commandments hast made me wiser ' than mine ' enemies : for ' they are ' ever ' with me.

99 I have more understanding ' than my ' teachers : for thy ' testimonies ' are my ' study.

100 I am wiser ' than the ' ag-ed : because I ' keep ' thy com-' mandments.

101 I have refrained my feet from every ' evil ' way : that ' I may ' keep thy ' word.

102 I have not shrunk ' from thy ' judgements : for ' thou' teachest ' me.

103 O how sweet are thy words ' unto my ' throat : yea sweeter than ' honey ' unto my ' mouth.

104 Through thy commandments I get ' under'standing : therefore I ' hate all ' evil ' ways.

DAY 26 MORNING

Vss 105 - 120

R. P. GOODENOUGH

203

THY word is a lantern ' unto my ' feet : and a ' light ' unto my ' paths.

106 I have sworn and am ' stedfastly ' purposed : to ' keep thy ' righteous ' judgements.

107 I am troubled a'bove ' measure : quicken me O Lord ac'cording ' to thy ' word.

108 Let the free-will offerings of my mouth please ' thee O ' Lord : and ' teach me ' thy ' judgements.

109 My soul is alway ' in my ' hand : yet do I ' not for'get thy ' law.

110 The ungodly have ' laid a ' snare for me : but yet I swerved ' not from ' thy com'mandments.

111 Thy testimonies have I claimed as mine ' heritage for'ever : and why?, they are the ' very ' joy of my ' heart.

* 112 I have applied my heart to ful'fil thy ' statutes ' alway : ' even ' unto the ' end.

———

I HATE them that imagine ' evil ' things : but thy ' law ' do I ' love.

114 Thou art my de'fence and ' shield : and my ' trust is ' in thy ' word.

115 Away from ' me ye ' wicked : I will keep the com'mandments ' of my ' God.

Vs 112

I have applied my heart to ful-   fil   thy   statutes   alway: ev - en un - to the end.

112 I have applied my heart to fulfil thy ' statutes ' alway : even ' un'to the ' end.

203

116 O stablish me according to thy word that ' I may ' live : and let me
not be disap'pointed ' of my ' hope.

117 Hold thou me up and ' I shall be ' safe : yea my delight shall be ' ever '
in thy ' statutes.

118 Thou hast trodden down all them that depart ' from thy ' statutes :
for they im'agine ' but de'ceit.

119 Thou puttest away all the ungodly of the ' earth like ' dross :
therefore I ' love ' thy ' testimonies.

120 My flesh trembleth for ' fear of ' thee : and I am a'fraid of ' thy '
judgements.

204

I DEAL with the thing that is ' lawful and ' right : O give me not over '
unto ' mine op'pressors.

122 Make thou thy servant to delight in ' that which is ' good : that the
proud ' do me ' no ' wrong.

123 Mine eyes are wasted away with looking ' for thy ' health : and for
the ' word of ' thy ' righteousness.

124 O deal with thy servant according unto thy ' loving ' mercy : and '
teach me ' thy ' statutes.

125 I am thy servant, O grant me ' under'standing : that ' I may '
know thy ' testimonies.

126 It is time for thee Lord to lay ' to thine ' hand : for ' they have de-'
stroyed thy ' law.

127 For I love ' thy com'mandments : above ' gold and ' precious ' stone.

128 Therefore hold I straight all ' thy com'mandments : and all false '
ways I ' utterly ab'hor.

———————

THY testimonies ' are ' wonderful : therefore ' doth my ' soul ' keep them.

130 When thy word ' goeth ' forth : it giveth light and under'standing '
unto the ' simple.

131 I opened my mouth and drew ' in my ' breath : for my de-'
light was in ' thy com'mandments.

132 O look thou upon me and be ' merciful ' unto me : as thou usest to do
unto ' those that ' love thy ' Name.

133 Order my ' steps in thy ' word : and so shall no wickedness '
have do'minion ' over me.

134 O deliver me from the wrongful ' dealings of ' men : and so shall I '
keep ' thy com'mandments.

135 Shew the light of thy countenance up'on thy ' servant : and '
teach me ' thy ' statutes.

136 Mine eyes gush ' out with ' water : because men ' keep not ' thy '
law.

———————

RIGHTEOUS art ' thou O ' Lord : and ' true is ' thy ' judgement.

138 The testimonies that thou ' hast com'manded : are ex'ceeding '
righteous and ' true.

139 My zeal hath ' even con'sumed me : because mine enemies '
have for'gotten thy ' words.

140 Thy word is ' tried to the ' uttermost : and thy ' servant ' loveth ' it.

141 I am small and of no ' repu'tation : yet do I ' not for-'
get thy com'mandments.

142 Thy righteousness is an ever ' lasting ' righteousness : and thy '
law ' is the ' truth.

143 Trouble and heaviness have taken ' hold up'on me . yet is my de-'
light in ' thy com'mandments.

144 The righteousness of thy testimonies is ' ever'lasting : O grant me
under'standing and ' I shall ' live.

DAY 26   EVENING

I CALL with my ' whole ' heart : hear me O Lord ' I will ' keep thy '
statutes.

146 Yea even unto thee ' do I ' call : help me and ' I shall ' keep thy '
testimonies.

147 Early in the morning do I ' cry unto ' thee : for ' in thy '
word is my ' trust.

148 Mine eyes prevent the ' night' watches : that I might be' occupied '
in thy ' words.

149 Hear my voice O Lord, according unto thy ' loving' kindness
quicken me ac'cording as ' thou art ' wont.

150 They draw nigh that of ' malice ' persecute me : and are ' far '
from thy ' law.

151 Be thou nigh at ' hand O ' Lord : for all ' thy com'mandments are '
true.

152 As concerning thy testimonies I have ' known long ' since : that
thou hast ' grounded ' them for ' ever.

O CONSIDER mine adversity ' and de'liver me : for I do ' not for'get thy
law.

154 Avenge thou my cause ' and de'liver me : quicken me ac'cording
to thy ' word.

155 Health is far ' from the un'godly : for ' they re'gard not thy
statutes.

156 Great is thy ' mercy O ' Lord : quicken ' me as ' thou art ' wont.

157 Many there are that ' trouble   me and ' persecute me : yet do I
not ' swerve ' from thy ' testimonies.

158 It grieveth me when I ' see the trans'gressors : be'cause they
keep not thy ' law.

159 Consider O Lord how I love ' thy com'mandments : O quicken me ac'cording · to thy ' loving ' kindness.

160 Thy word is true from ' ever'lasting : all the judgements of thy righteousness en'dure for ' ever'more.

Vss 161 - 176   E. J. HOPKINS

PRINCES have persecuted me with'out a ' cause : but my heart ' standeth in ' awe of thy ' word.

162 I am as ' glad of thy ' word : as one that ' findeth ' great ' spoils.

163 As for lies I ' hate and ab'hor them : but thy ' law ' do I ' love.

164 Seven times a ' day do I ' praise thee : be'cause of thy ' righteous ' judgements.

165 Great is the peace that they have who ' love thy ' law : and they are ' not of 'fended ' at it.

166 Lord I have looked for thy ' saving ' health : and done ' after ' thy com'mandments.

167 My soul hath ' kept thy ' testimonies : and ' lov-ed ' them ex-' ceedingly.

168 I have kept thy com'mandments and ' testimonies : for ' all my ' ways are be'fore thee.

LET my complaint come before ' thee O ' Lord : give me understanding ac'cording ' to thy ' word.

170 Let my supplication ' come be'fore thee : deliver me ac'cording ' to thy ' word.

171 My lips shall ' speak of thy ' praise : when thou hast ' taught me ' thy ' statutes.

172 Yea my tongue shall ' sing of thy ' word : for ' all thy com-' mandments are ' righteous.

173 Let thine ' hand ' help me : for I have ' chosen ' thy com-'
mandments.

174 I have longed for thy saving ' health O ' Lord : and in thy ' law is '
my de'light.

175 O let my soul live and ' it shall ' praise thee : and thy '
judgements ' shall ' help me.

176 I have gone astray like a ' sheep that is ' lost : O seek thy servant
for I ' do not for'get thy com'mandments.

DAY 27   MORNING

PSALM 120

*   When I ' was in ' trouble ' I called upon the ' Lord : and ' he
heard me.

2 Deliver my soul O Lord from'lying'lips : and ' from a de'ceitful
tongue.

Ps. 120. vs. 1 When I was in trouble I called up'on the ' Lord : and ' he ' heard ' me.

3 What reward shall be given or done unto thee thou ' false ' tongue :
even mighty and sharp ' arrows with ' hot burning ' coals.

4 Woe is me that I am constrained to ' dwell with ' Mesech : and to
have my habitation a'mong the ' tents of ' Kedar.

5 My soul hath long ' dwelt a'mong them : that are ' enemies ' unto '
peace.

6 I labour for peace, but when I speak unto ' them there'of : they '
make them ' ready to ' battle.

PSALM 121

I WILL lift up mine eyes ' unto the ' hills : from ' whence ' cometh my '
help.

2 My help cometh even ' from the ' Lord : who ' hath made '
heaven and ' earth.

3 He will not suffer thy ' foot to be ' moved : and he that '
keepeth thee ' will not ' sleep.

4 Behold he that ' keepeth ' Israel : shall ' neither ' slumber nor '
sleep.

5 The Lord himself ' is thy ' keeper : the Lord is thy de'fence upon '
thy right ' hand;

*   6 So that the ' sun shall not ' burn thee by ' day : ' neither the '
moon by ' night.

7 The Lord shall preserve thee from ' all ' evil : yea it is even he '
that shall ' keep thy ' soul.

8 The Lord shall preserve thy going out and thy ' coming ' in : from
this time ' forth for ' ever'more.

's. 121. vs. 6 So that the sun shall not burn ' thee by ' day : neither the ' moon ' by ' night.

PSALM 122

J. ROBINSON

209

I WAS glad when they said ' unto ' me : We will ' go into the '
house of the ' Lord.

* 2 Our ' feet shall ' stand ' in thy ' gates : ' O Je'rusalem.

3 Jerusalem is ' built as a ' city : that is at ' unity ' in it'self.

4 For thither the tribes go up, even the ' tribes of the ' Lord : to testify
unto Israel, to give thanks ' unto the ' Name of the ' Lord.

2nd   5 For there is the ' seat of ' judgement : even the ' seat of the '
Part   house of ' David.

6 O pray for the ' peace of Je'rusalem : they shall ' prosper that ' love '
thee.

7 Peace be with'in thy ' walls : and ' plenteousness with'in thy '
palaces.

8 For my brethren and com'panions' ' sakes : I will ' wish
thee pros'perity.

9 Yea because of the house of the ' Lord our ' God : I will ' seek to
do thee ' good.

Our feet shall stand in thy gates: O Je - rusalem.

Ps. 122. vs. 2 Our feet shall stand ' in thy ' gates : O ' – Je'rusa'lem.

PSALM 123

210

T. PYMAR

UNTO thee lift I ' up mine ' eyes : O thou that ' dwellest ' in the ' heavens.

2 Behold, even as the eyes of servants look unto the hand of their masters, and as the eyes of a maiden unto the ' hand of her ' mistress : even so our eyes wait upon the Lord our God, until ' he have ' mercy up'on us.

3 Have mercy upon us, O Lord have ' mercy up'on us : for ' we are ' utterly des'pised.

4 Our soul is filled with the scornful re'proof of the ' wealthy : and with the de'spitefulness ' of the ' proud.

PSALM 124

211

Vss 1 - 4

J. HARRISON

IF the Lord himself had not been on our side, now may ' Israel ' say : if the Lord himself had not been on our side when ' men rose ' up a'gainst us;

2 They had swallowed ' us up ' quick : when they were so ' wrathfully dis'pleas-ed ' at us.

3 Yea the ' waters had ' drowned us : and the ' stream had gone ' over our ' soul.

4 The deep ' waters · of the ' proud : had gone ' even ' over our ' soul.

Change to Chant 212 overleaf

5 But praised ' be the ' Lord : who hath not given us over for a ' prey '
   unto their ' teeth.

6 Our soul is escaped, even as a bird out of the ' snare of the ' fowler :
   the snare is ' broken and ' we · are de'livered.

2nd   7 Our help standeth in the ' Name of the ' Lord : who hath ' made '
Part   heaven and ' earth.

PSALM 125

THEY that put their trust in the Lord shall be even ' as the mount '
   Sion : which may not be removed but ' standeth ' fast for ' ever.

2 The hills stand a'bout Je'rusalem : even so standeth the Lord round
   about his people, from this time ' forth for ' ever'more.

2nd   3 For the rod of the ungodly, cometh not into the ' lot of the ' righteous
Part   lest the righteous ' put their ' hand unto ' wickedness.

4 Do ' well O ' Lord : unto those that are ' good and ' true of ' heart.

5 As for such as turn back into their ' own ' wickedness : the Lord '
   shall lead them forth with the evil-doers, but ' peace shall '
   be upon ' Israel.

DAY 27 EVENING

PSALM 126

J. TURLE

214

WHEN the Lord turned again the cap'tivity of ' Sion : then were we '
like unto ' them that ' dream.

2 Then was our mouth ' filled with ' laughter : and ' our ' tongue with '
joy.

3 Then said they a'mong the ' heathen : The ' Lord hath done '
great things ' for them.

4 Yea, the Lord hath done great things ' for us al'ready : where'of '
we re'joice.

5 Turn our cap'tivity O ' Lord : as the ' rivers ' in the ' south.

6 They that ' sow in ' tears : shall ' reap ' in ' joy.

2nd
Part   7 He that now goeth on his way weeping, and beareth ' forth good '
seed : shall doubtless come again with joy and ' bring his ' sheaves '
with him.

PSALM 127

215

EXCEPT the Lord ' build the ' house : their labour ' is but ' lost that build it.

2 Except the Lord ' keep the ' city : the watchman ' waketh but in ' vain.

3 It is but lost labour that ye haste to rise up early, and so late take rest, and eat the ' bread of ' carefulness : for so he giveth his be'lov-ed ' sleep.

4 Lo children and the ' fruit of the ' womb : are an heritage and gift that ' cometh ' of the ' Lord.

5 Like as the arrows in the ' hand of the ' giant : even so ' are the young ' children.

6 Happy is the man that hath his quiver ' full of ' them : they shall not be ashamed, when they speak with their ' enemies ' in the gate.

PSALM 128

216

BLESSED are all they that ' fear the ' Lord : and ' walk in ' his ' ways.

2 For thou shalt eat the labours ' of thine ' hands : O well is thee and happy ' shalt thou ' be.

3 Thy wife shall be as the ' fruitful ' vine : up'on the ' walls of thine house.

210

* 4 Thy children ' like the ' olive ' branches : ' round a'bout thy ' table.

5 Lo thus shall the ' man be ' blessed : that ' fear'eth the ' Lord.

6 The Lord from out of Sion shall ' so ' bless thee : that thou shalt see Jerusalem in prosperity ' all thy ' life ' long.

2nd 7 Yea that thou shalt see thy ' children's ' children : and '
Part   peace up'on ' Israel.

PSALM 129

T. A. WALMISLEY

17

MANY a time have they fought against me from my ' youth ' up : may ' Israel ' now ' say.

2 Yea many a time have they vexed me from my ' youth ' up : but they have ' not pre'vailed a'gainst me.

3 The plowers plowed up'on my ' back : and ' made ' long ' furrows.

4 But the ' righteous ' Lord : hath hewn the ' snares of · the un-' godly in ' pieces.

5 Let them be confounded and ' turned ' backward : as many as have ' evil ' will at ' Sion.

6 Let them be even as the grass growing up'on the ' house-tops : which withereth a'fore it be ' pluck-ed ' up;

7 Whereof the mower filleth ' not his ' hand : neither he that bindeth'up the ' sheaves his ' bosom.

8 So that they who go by, say not so much as The ' Lord ' prosper you : we wish you good ' luck in the ' Name of the ' Lord.

Ps. 128, Vs 4

Thy children like the olive - branches: round a - bout thy table.

Ps. 128. vs 4 Thy children like the ' olive ' branches : round ' – a'bout thy ' table.

PSALM 130

218

Slow

p   OUT of the deep have I called unto ' thee O ' Lord : Lord ' hear ' my voice.

2   O let thine ears con'sider ' well : the ' voice of ' my com'plaint.

3   If thou Lord wilt be extreme to mark what is ' done a'miss : O Lord who ' may a'bide it?

4   For there is ' mercy with ' thee : therefore ' shalt ' thou be ' feared

5   I look for the Lord, my ' soul doth ' wait for him : in his ' word is my ' trust.

6   My soul fleeth ' unto the ' Lord : before the morning watch, I sa be'fore the ' morning ' watch.

219

f   7   O Israel trust in the Lord, for with the Lord ' there is ' mercy : an with ' him is ' plenteous re'demption.

8   And he shall re'deem ' Israel : from ' all ' his ' sins.

PSALM 131

Slow

p LORD I am ' not high'minded : I have ' no ' proud ' looks.

2 I do not exercise myself in ' great ' matters : which ' are too ' high for ' me.

3 But I refrain my soul and keep it low, like as a child that is wean-ed ' from his ' mother : yea my soul is even ' as a ' wean-ed ' child.

f 4 O Israel ' trust in the ' Lord : from this time ' forth for ' ever'more.

DAY 28 MORNING

PSALM 132

LORD re'member ' David : and ' all ' his ' trouble;

2 How he sware ' unto the ' Lord : and vowed a vow unto the Al'mighty ' God of ' Jacob;

3 I will not come within the tabernacle ' of mine ' house : nor ' climb up ' into my ' bed;

4 I will not suffer mine eyes to sleep nor mine ' eye-lids to ' slumber : neither the temples of my ' head to ' take · any ' rest;

2nd 5 Until I find out a place for the ' temple of the ' Lord : an habitation
Part   for the ' mighty ' God of ' Jacob.

6 Lo we heard of the ' same at ' Ephrata : and ' found it ' in the '
  wood.

7 We will go ' into his ' tabernacle : and fall low on our ' knees be-'
  fore his ' footstool.

8 Arise O Lord ' into thy ' resting-place : thou and the ' ark of ' thy '
  strength.

9 Let thy priests be ' clothed with ' righteousness : and let thy ' saints '
  sing with ' joyfulness.

10 For thy servant ' David's ' sake : turn not away the ' presence of '
   thine A'nointed.

11 The Lord hath made a faithful ' oath unto ' David : and he '
   shall not ' shrink ' from it;

12 Of the fruit ' of thy ' body : shall I ' set up'on thy ' seat.

13 If thy children will keep my covenant, and my testimonies that '
   I shall ' learn them : their children also shall sit upon thy '
   seat for ' ever'more.

14 For the Lord hath chosen Sion to be an habitation ' for him'self : he
   hath ' long-ed ' for ' her.

15 This shall be my ' rest for'ever : here will I dwell, for I
   have a de'light there'in.

16 I will bless her ' victuals with ' increase : and will ' satisfy her '
   poor with ' bread.

17 I will deck her ' priests with ' health : and her ' saints shall re-'
joice and ' sing.

18 There shall I make the horn of ' David to ' flourish : I have ordained
a ' lantern for ' mine A'nointed.

19 As for his enemies, I shall ' clothe them with ' shame : but upon
him'self shall his ' crown ' flourish.

PSALM 133

BEHOLD how good and joyful a ' thing it ' is : brethren to '
dwell to'gether in ' unity!

2 It is like the precious ointment upon the head, that ran down '
unto the ' beard : even unto Aaron's beard, and went '
down to the ' skirts of his ' clothing.

3 Like as the ' dew of ' Hermon : which fell up'on the ' hill of ' Sion.

4 For there the Lord ' promised his ' blessing : and ' life for '
ever'more.

PSALM 134

BEHOLD now ' praise the ' Lord : all ye ' servants ' of the ' Lord;

2 Ye that by night stand in the ' house of the ' Lord : even in the
courts of the ' house of ' our ' God.

3 Lift up your hands ' in the ' sanctuary : and ' praise ' – the ' Lord.

Unison 4 The Lord that made ' heaven and ' earth : give thee ' blessing '
out of ' Sion.

215

PSALM 135

J. TURL[

226

O PRAISE the Lord, laud ye the ' Name of the ' Lord : praise it O ye '
    servants ' of the ' Lord;

2 Ye that stand in the ' house of the ' Lord : in the ' courts of the '
    house of our ' God.

3 O praise the Lord for the ' Lord is ' gracious : O sing praises unt(
    his ' Name for ' it is ' lovely.

4 For why? the Lord hath chosen Jacob ' unto him'self : and Israel
    for his ' own pos'session.

2nd   5 For I know that the ' Lord is ' great : and that our Lord ' is a-
Part   bove all ' gods.

6 Whatsoever the Lord pleased, that did he in heaven ' and in ' earth
    and in the sea ' and in ' all deep ' places.

7 He bringeth forth the clouds from the ' ends of the ' world : an(
    sendeth forth lightnings with the rain, bringing the ' winds
    out of his ' treasures.

8 He smote the ' first-born of ' Egypt : both of ' man ' and ' beast.

9 He hath sent tokens and wonders into the midst of thee, O thou
    land of ' Egypt : upon ' Pharaoh and ' all his ' servants.

10 He smote ' divers ' nations : and ' slew ' mighty ' kings;

11 Sehon king of the Amorites, and Og the ' king of ' Basan : and
    all the ' kingdoms of ' Canaan;

2nd   12 And gave their land to ' be an ' heritage : even an heritage ' unto
Part   Israel his ' people.

13 Thy Name O Lord en'dureth for'ever : so doth thy memoria[
    O Lord, from one gene'ration ' to ano'ther.

14 For the Lord will a'venge his ' people : and be ' gracious ' unto his
    servants.

15 As for the images of the heathen, they are but ' silver and ' gold
    the ' work of ' men's ' hands.

16 They have ' mouths and ' speak not : eyes ' have they ' but they ' see not.

17 They have ears and ' yet they ' hear not : neither is there ' any ' breath in their ' mouths.

18 They that make them are like ' unto ' them : and so are all ' they that ' put their ' trust in them.

19 Praise the Lord ye ' house of ' Israel : praise the ' Lord ye ' house of ' Aaron.

20 Praise the Lord ye ' house of ' Levi : ye that fear the ' Lord ' praise the ' Lord.

2nd Pt. 21 Praised be the Lord ' out of ' Sion : who ' dwelleth ' at Je'rusalem.

DAY 28   EVENING
PSALM 136

Single Chant

227

O GIVE thanks unto the Lord for ' he is ' gracious : and his ' mercy en'dureth for ' ever.

2 O give thanks unto the God of ' all ' gods : for his ' mercy en-' dureth for ' ever.

3 O thank the Lord of ' all ' lords : for his ' mercy en'dureth for ' ever.

4 Who only ' doeth great ' wonders : for his ' mercy en'dureth for ' ever.

5 Who by his excellent wisdom ' made the ' heavens : for his ' mercy en'dureth for ' ever.

6 Who laid out the earth a'bove the ' waters : for his ' mercy en-' dureth for ' ever.

217

7 Who hath ' made great ' lights : for his ' mercy en'dureth for ' ever;

8 The sun to ' rule the ' day : for his ' mercy en'dureth for ' ever;

9 The moon and the stars to ' govern the ' night : for his ' mercy en'dureth for ' ever.

10 Who smote Egypt ' with their ' first-born : for his ' mercy en-' dureth for ' ever;

11 And brought out Israel ' from a'mong them : for his ' mercy en'dureth for ' ever;

12 With a mighty hand and ' stretched out ' arm : for his ' mercy en'dureth for ' ever.

13 Who divided the Red sea in ' two ' parts : for his ' mercy en-' dureth for ' ever;

14 And made Israel to ' go through the ' midst of it : for his ' mercy en'dureth for ' ever.

15 But as for Pharoah and his host, he overthrew them in the ' Red ' sea : for his ' mercy en'dureth for ' ever.

227

16 Who led his people ' through the ' wilderness : for his '
mercy en'dureth for ' ever.

17 Who smote ' great ' kings : for his ' mercy en'dureth for ' ever;

18 Yea and slew ' mighty ' kings : for his ' mercy en'dureth for ' ever;

19 Sehon ' king of the ' Amorites : for his ' mercy en'dureth for ' ever;

20 And Og the ' king of ' Basan : for his ' mercy en'dureth for ' ever;

21 And gave away their ' land · for an ' heritage : for his '
mercy en'dureth for ' ever;

22 Even for an heritage unto ' Israel his ' servant : for his '
mercy en'dureth for ' ever.

23 Who remembered us when we ' were in ' trouble : for his '
mercy en'dureth for ' ever;

24 And hath delivered us ' from our ' enemies : for his '
mercy en'dureth for ' ever.

25 Who giveth food to ' all ' flesh : for his ' mercy en'dureth for ' ever.

227

26 O give thanks unto the ' God of ' heaven : for his ' mercy en-'
dureth for ' ever.

27 O give thanks unto the ' Lord of ' lords : for his ' mercy en-'
dureth for ' ever.

PSALM 137

W. R. BEXFIELD

228

Slow. Single Chant.

p BY the waters of Babylon we sat ' down and ' wept : when we re'membered ' thee O ' Sion.

2 As for our harps we ' hanged them ' up : upon the ' trees that ' are there'in.

3 For they that led us away captive required of us then a song, and melody ' in our ' heaviness : Sing us ' one of the ' songs of ' Sion.

* 4 How shall we ' sing the ' Lord's ' song : ' in a ' strange ' land?

5 If I forget thee ' O Je'rusalem : let my right ' hand for'get her ' cunning.

6 If I do not remember thee, let my tongue cleave to the ' roof of my ' mouth : yea if I prefer not Je'rusalem ' in my ' mirth.

[7 Remember the children of Edom O Lord, in the ' day of Je'rusalem : how they said, Down with it, down with it, ' even ' to the ' ground.

8 O daughter of Babylon ' wasted with ' misery : yea happy shall he be that rewardeth thee, as ' thou hast ' serv-ed ' us.

9 Blessed shall he be that ' taketh thy ' children : and ' throweth them a'gainst the ' stones.]

How shall we sing the Lord's song: in a strange land?

4 How shall we sing the ' Lord's ' song : in ' – a ' strange ' land?

PSALM 138

W. HAYES

229

I WILL give thanks unto thee O Lord, with my ' whole ' heart : even
before the gods will I sing ' praise ' unto ' thee.

2 I will worship toward thy holy temple and praise thy Name, because
of thy loving'kindness and ' truth : for thou hast magnified thy
Name and thy ' word a'bove ' all things.

3 When I called upon ' thee/thou ' heardest me : and enduedst my '
soul with ' much ' strength.

4 All the kings of the earth shall ' praise thee O ' Lord : for they have '
heard the ' words of thy ' mouth.

5 Yea they shall sing in the ' ways of the ' Lord : that great is the '
glory ' of the ' Lord.

6 For though the Lord be high, yet hath he respect ' unto the ' lowly :
as for the proud, he beholdeth ' them a'far ' off.

7 Though I walk in the midst of trouble, yet shalt ' thou re'fresh me :
thou shalt stretch forth thy hand upon the furiousness of mine
enemies, and thy ' right ' hand shall ' save me.

8 The Lord shall make good his loving'kindness ' toward me : yea thy
mercy O Lord endureth for ever, despise not then the '
works of thine ' own ' hands.

DAY 29   MORNING
PSALM 139

R. P. GOODENOUGH

230

O LORD thou hast searched me ' out and ' known me : thou knowest
my down-sitting and mine up-rising, thou understandest my '
thoughts ' long be'fore.

2 Thou art about my path and a'bout my ' bed : and ' spiest out '
all my ' ways.

R. P. GOODENOUGH

230

3 For lo there is not a word ' in my ' tongue : but thou O Lord '
knowest it ' alto'gether.

4 Thou hast fashioned me be'hind and be'fore : and ' laid thine '
hand up'on me.

2nd   5 Such knowledge is too wonderful and ' excellent ' for me : I '
Part   cannot at'tain unto ' it.

6 Whither shall I go then ' from thy ' Spirit : or whither shall I '
go then ' from thy ' presence?

7 If I climb up into heaven ' thou art ' there : if I go down to hell '
thou art ' there ' also.

8 If I take the ' wings of the ' morning : and remain in the ' uttermost '
parts of the ' sea;

9 Even there also shall ' thy hand ' lead me : and ' thy right '
hand shall ' hold me.

10 If I say, Peradventure the ' darkness shall ' cover me : then shall
my ' night be ' turned to ' day.

11 Yea the darkness is no darkness with thee, but the night is as '
clear as the ' day : the darkness and light to ' thee are '
both a'like.

12 For my ' reins are ' thine : thou hast covered me ' in my ' mother's '
womb.

13 I will give thanks unto thee, for I am fearfully and ' wonderfully '
made : marvellous are thy works, and that my ' soul '
knoweth right ' well.

14 My bones are not ' hid from ' thee : though I be made secretly, and '
fashioned be'neath in the ' earth.

15 Thine eyes did see my substance yet ' being un'perfect : and in thy
book were ' all my ' members ' written;

2nd   16 Which day by ' day were ' fashioned : when as yet ' there was '
Part   none of ' them.

17 How dear are thy counsels unto ' me O ' God : O how ' great is the '
sum of ' them!

18 If I tell them, they are more in number ' than the ' sand : when I
wake up ' I am ' present with ' thee.

19 Wilt thou not slay the ' wicked O ' God : depart from ' me ye '
blood-thirsty ' men.

20 For they speak un'righteously a'gainst thee : and thine enemies '
take thy ' Name in ' vain.

21 Do not I hate them O Lord that ' hate ' thee : and am not I grieved
with those that ' rise ' up a'gainst thee?

22 Yea I ' hate them right ' sore : even as ' though they ' were mine '
enemies.

23 Try me O God, and seek the ' ground of my ' heart : prove me '
and ex'amine my ' thoughts.

24 Look well if there be any way of ' wickedness ' in me : and lead me
in the ' way ' ever'lasting.

PSALM 140

G. WOODWARD

231

DELIVER me O Lord from the ' evil ' man : and preserve me ' from the '
wicked ' man.

2 Who imagine mischief ' in their ' hearts : and stir up ' strife '
all the day ' long.

3 They have sharpened their tongues ' like a ' serpent : adders' '
poison is ' under their ' lips.

4 Keep me O Lord from the ' hands of · the un'godly : preserve me
from the wicked men, who are purposed to ' over'throw my '
goings.

2nd
Part
5 The proud have laid a snare for me, and spread a net a'broad with '
cords : yea and set ' traps in ' my ' way.

6 I said unto the Lord, Thou ' art my ' God : hear the ' voice of my ' prayers O ' Lord.

7 O Lord God, thou strength ' of my ' health : thou hast covered my ' head in the ' day of ' battle.

8 Let not the ungodly have his de'sire O ' Lord : let not his mischievous imagination prosper ' lest they ' be too ' proud.

[9 Let the mischief of their own lips fall upon the ' head of ' them : that ' compass ' me a'bout.

10 Let hot burning coals ' fall up'on them : let them be cast into the fire and into the pit, that they ' never rise ' up a'gain.]

11 A man full of words shall not prosper up'on the ' earth : evil shall hunt the wicked ' person to ' over'throw him.

12 Sure I am that the Lord will a'venge the ' poor : and main'tain the ' cause of the ' helpless.

13 The righteous also shall give thanks ' unto thy ' Name : and the just shall con'tinue in ' thy ' sight.

PSALM 141

LORD I call upon thee, haste thee ' unto ' me : and consider my voice when I ' cry ' unto ' thee.

2 Let my prayer be set forth in thy sight ' as the ' incense : and let the lifting up of my hands ' be an ' evening ' sacrifice.

3 Set a watch O Lord be'fore my ' mouth : and ' keep the ' door of my ' lips.

4 O let not mine heart be inclined to any ' evil ' thing : let me not be occupied in ungodly works with the men that work wickedness, lest I ' eat of such ' things as ' please them.

* 5 Let the righteous ' rather ' smite me ' friendly : ' and re'prove ' me.

6 But let not their precious balms ' break my ' head : yea I will pray ' yet a'gainst their ' wickedness.

[7 Let their judges be overthrown in ' stony ' places : that they may hear my ' words for ' they are ' sweet.

8 Our bones lie scattered be'fore the ' pit : like as when one breaketh and heweth ' wood up'on the ' earth.]

9 But mine eyes look unto thee O ' Lord ' God : in thee is my trust O ' cast not ' out my ' soul.

10 Keep me from the snare that ' they have ' laid for me : and from the ' traps of the ' wicked ' doers.

2nd Part 11 Let the ungodly fall into their own ' nets to'gether : and ' let me ' ever es'cape them.

DAY 29 EVENING

PSALM 142

Slow

I CRIED unto the Lord ' with my ' voice : yea even unto the Lord did I ' make my ' suppli'cation.

2 I poured out my com'plaints be'fore him : and ' shewed him ' of my ' trouble.

5 Let the righteous rather ' smite me ' friendly : and ' – re'prove ' me.

233

3 When my spirit was in heaviness thou ' knewest my ' path : in the way wherein I walked have they ' privily ' laid a ' snare for me.

4 I looked also upon my ' right ' hand : and saw there was ' no man ' that would ' know me.

2nd Pt. 5 I had no place to ' flee ' unto : and no man ' car-ed ' for my ' soul.

6 I cried unto thee O ' Lord and ' said : Thou art my hope, and my portion ' in the ' land of the ' living.

7 Consider ' my com'plaint : for I am ' brought ' very ' low.

8 O deliver me ' from my ' persecutors : for ' they are too ' strong for ' me.

9 Bring my soul out of prison, that I may give thanks ' unto thy ' Name : which thing if thou wilt grant me, then shall the righteous re'sort ' unto my ' company.

PSALM 143

234

HEAR my prayer O Lord, and consider ' my de'sire : hearken unto me for thy ' truth and ' righteousness' ' sake.

2 And enter not into judgement ' with thy ' servant : for in thy sight shall ' no man ' living be ' justified.

3 For the enemy hath persecuted my soul, he hath smitten my life ' down to the ' ground : he hath laid me in the darkness, as the ' men that have ' been long ' dead.

4 Therefore is my spirit ' vexed with'in me : and my ' heart with-'in me is ' desolate.

5 Yet do I remember the time past, I muse upon ' all thy ' works : yea, I exercise myself in the ' works of ' thy ' hands.

6 I stretch forth my hands ' unto ' thee : my soul gaspeth unto thee ' as a ' thirsty ' land.

7 Hear me O Lord and that soon, for my spirit ' waxeth ' faint : hide not thy face from me, lest I be like unto them that go ' down ' into the ' pit.

8 O let me hear thy loving-kindness betimes in the morning, for in thee ' is my ' trust : shew thou me the way that I should walk in, for I lift up my ' soul ' unto ' thee.

9 Deliver me O Lord ' from mine ' enemies : for I flee ' unto ' thee to ' hide me.

10 Teach me to do the thing that pleaseth thee, for thou ' art my ' God : let thy loving Spirit lead me forth ' into the ' land of ' righteousness.

11 Quicken me O Lord for thy ' Name's ' sake : and for thy righteous-ness' sake bring my ' soul ' out of ' trouble.

12 And of thy goodness ' slay mine ' enemes : and destroy all them that vex my soul, for ' I am ' thy ' servant.

DAY 30   MORNING

PSALM 144

J. RANDALL

235

BLESSED be the ' Lord my ' strength : who teacheth my hands to war ' and my ' fingers to ' fight;

2 My hope and my fortress, my castle and deliverer, my defender in ' whom I ' trust : who subdueth my ' people ' that is ' under me.

3 Lord what is man, that thou hast such respect ' unto ' him : or the son of man, that thou ' so re'gardest ' him?

J. RANDALL

235

4 Man is like a ' thing of ' nought : his time ' passeth a'way like a '
   shadow.

5 Bow thy heavens O Lord ' and come ' down : touch the '
   mountains and ' they shall ' smoke.

6 Cast forth thy ' lightning and ' tear them : shoot out thine ' arrows '
   and con'sume them.

7 Send down thine hand ' from a'bove : deliver me and take me out of
   the great waters, from the ' hand of ' strange ' children;

8 Whose mouth ' talketh of ' vanity : and their right hand ' is a right '
   hand of ' wickedness.

9 I will sing a new song unto ' thee O ' God : and sing praises unto
   thee up'on a ' ten-stringed ' lute.

10 Thou hast given victory ' unto ' kings : and hast delivered David
   thy servant from the ' peril ' of the ' sword.

2nd   11 Save me and deliver me from the hand of ' strange ' children :
Part   whose mouth talketh of vanity, and their right hand ' is a right '
   hand of in'iquity.

12 That our sons may grow up as the ' young ' plants : and that our
   daughters may be as the polished ' corners ' of the ' temple.

13 That our garners may be full and plenteous, with all ' manner of '
   store : that our sheep may bring forth thousands, and ten '
   thousands ' in our ' streets.

14 That our oxen may be strong to labour, that there be ' no de'cay :
   no leading into captivity, and no com'plaining ' in our ' streets.

15 Happy are the people that are in ' such a ' case : yea blessed are the
   people who have the ' Lord for ' their ' God.

PSALM 145

T. NORRIS

236

I WILL magnify thee O ' God my ' King : and I will praise thy '
  Name for ' ever and ' ever.

2 Every day will I give thanks ' unto ' thee : and praise thy '
  Name for ' ever and ' ever.

3 Great is the Lord, and marvellous worthy ' to be ' praised : there '
  is no ' end of his ' greatness.

4 One generation shall praise thy works ' unto an'other : and de'clare '
  thy ' power.

5 As for me, I will be talking ' of thy ' worship : thy glory thy '
  praise and ' wondrous ' works;

6 So that men shall speak of the might of thy ' marvellous ' acts : and
  I will ' also ' tell of thy ' greatness.

2nd   7 The memorial of thine abundant kindness ' shall be ' shewed : and '
Part   men shall ' sing of thy ' righteousness.

8 The Lord is ' gracious and ' merciful : long-suffering ' and of ' great '
  goodness.

9 The Lord is loving ' unto ' every man : and his mercy is ' over '
  all his ' works.

10 All thy works praise ' thee O ' Lord : and thy ' saints give '
   thanks unto ' thee.

11 They shew the glory ' of thy ' kingdom : and ' talk of ' thy ' power;

12 That thy power thy glory and mightiness ' of thy ' kingdom : might
   be ' known ' unto ' men.

13 Thy kingdom is an ever'lasting ' kingdom : and thy dominion
   en'dureth through'out all ' ages.

14 The Lord upholdeth all ' such as ' fall : and lifteth up all ' those '
   that are ' down.

T. NORRIS

236

15 The eyes of all wait upon ' thee O ' Lord : and thou givest them
their ' meat in ' due ' season.

16 Thou openest ' thine ' hand : and fillest ' all things ' living with '
plenteousness.

17 The Lord is righteous in ' all his ' ways : and ' holy in ' all his '
works.

18 The Lord is nigh unto all them that ' call up'on him : yea all such
as ' call up'on him ' faithfully.

19 He will fulfil the desire of ' them that ' fear him : he also will hear
their ' cry ' and will ' help them.

20 The Lord preserveth all ' them that ' love him : but scattereth
a'broad ' all the un'godly.

21 My mouth shall speak the ' praise · of the ' Lord : and let all flesh
give thanks unto his holy ' Name for ' ever and ' ever.

PSALM 146

J. NARES

237

PRAISE the Lord O my soul, while I live will I ' praise the ' Lord : yea,
as long as I have any being, I will sing ' praises ' unto my ' God.

2 O put not your trust in princes, nor in any ' child of ' man : for there '
is no ' help in ' them.

3 For when the breath of man goeth forth, he shall turn a'gain to his '
earth : and then ' all his ' thoughts ' perish.

4 Blessed is he that hath the God of Jacob ' for his ' help : and whose
hope is ' in the ' Lord his ' God;

5 Who made heaven and earth, the sea and all that ' therein ' is : who ' keepeth his ' promise for ' ever;

6 Who helpeth them to right that ' suffer ' wrong : who ' feed'eth the ' hungry.

7 The Lord looseth men ' out of ' prison : the Lord giveth ' sight ' to the ' blind.

8 The Lord helpeth ' them that are ' fallen : the Lord ' careth ' for the ' righteous.

9 The Lord careth for the strangers, he defendeth the ' fatherless and ' widow : as for the way of the ungodly he ' turneth it ' upside ' down.

10 The Lord thy God O Sion, shall be King for ' ever'more : and through'out all ' gene'rations.

DAY 30 EVENING

PSALM 147

238

O PRAISE the Lord, for it is a good thing to sing praises ' unto our ' God : yea a joyful and pleasant ' thing it ' is to be ' thankful.

2 The Lord doth build ' up Je'rusalem : and gather to'gether the ' out-casts of ' Israel.

3 He healeth those that are ' broken in ' heart : and giveth ' medicine to ' heal their ' sickness.

4 He telleth the ' number · of the ' stars : and ' calleth them ' all by their ' names.

5 Great is our Lord and ' great is his ' power : yea ' and his ' wisdom is ' infinite.

6 The Lord setteth ' up the ' meek : and bringeth the un'godly ' down to the ' ground.

7 O sing unto the ' Lord with ' thanksgiving : sing praises upon the ' harp ' unto our ' God;

238

H. ALDRICH

8 Who covereth the heaven with clouds, and prepareth ' rain for the ' earth : and maketh the grass to grow upon the mountains, and ' herb · for the ' use of ' men;

9 Who giveth fodder ' unto the ' cattle : and feedeth the young ' ravens that ' call up'on him.

10 He hath no pleasure in the ' strength of an ' horse : neither delighteth ' he in ' any man's ' legs.

2nd 11 But the Lord's delight is in ' them that ' fear him : and ' put their '
Part trust in his ' mercy.

12 Praise the Lord ' O Je'rusalem : praise thy ' God ' O ' Sion.

13 For he hath made fast the ' bars of thy ' gates : and hath ' blessed thy ' children with'in thee.

14 He maketh ' peace in thy ' borders : and filleth thee ' with the ' flour of ' wheat.

15 He sendeth forth his commandment up'on ' earth : and his word ' runneth ' very ' swiftly.

16 He giveth ' snow like ' wool : and scattereth the ' hoar'frost like ' ashes.

17 He casteth forth his ' ice like ' morsels : who is ' able to a'bide his ' frost?

18 He sendeth out his ' word and ' melteth them : he bloweth with his wind ' and the ' waters ' flow.

19 He sheweth his word ' unto ' Jacob : his statutes and ' ordinances ' unto ' Israel.

2nd 20 He hath not dealt so with ' any ' nation : neither have the heathen '
Part knowledge ' of his ' laws.

PSALM 148

S. H. NICHOLSON

239

O PRAISE the ' Lord of ' heaven : praise him ' in the ' height.

2 Praise him all ye ' angels of ' his : praise him ' all his ' host.

3 Praise him ' sun and ' moon : praise him all ye ' stars and ' light.

4 Praise him ' all ye ' heavens : and ye waters that are a'bove the ' heavens.

5 Let them praise the ' Name of the ' Lord : for he spake the word and they were made, he commanded and they ' were cre'ated.

6 He hath made them fast for ' ever and ' ever : he hath given them a law which shall ' not be ' broken.

7 Praise the ' Lord upon ' earth : ye dragons and ' all ' deeps;

8 Fire and hail ' snow and ' vapours : wind and storm ful'filling his ' word;

9 Mountains and ' all ' hills : fruitful trees and ' all ' cedars;

10 Beasts and ' all ' cattle : worms and ' feathered ' fowls;

11 Kings of the earth and ' all ' people : princes and all judges ' of the ' world;

12 Young ' men and ' maidens : old ' men and ' children.

13 Praise the ' Name · of the ' Lord : for his Name only is excellent, and his praise above ' heaven and ' earth.

14 He shall exalt the ' horn of his ' people : all his ' saints shall ' praise him.

2nd Pt. 15 Even the ' children of ' Israel : even the people that ' serveth ' him.

Glory be to the Father, and ' to the ' Son : and to the ' Holy ' Ghost.

As it was in the beginning, is now and ' ever ' shall be : world without end. ' A'men.

alternative chant overleaf

PSALM 148

240

O PRAISE the ' Lord of ' heaven : praise ' him ' in the ' height.

2 Praise him all ye ' angels of ' his : praise ' him ' all his ' host.

3 Praise him ' sun and ' moon : praise him ' all ye ' stars and ' light.

4 Praise him ' all ye ' heavens : and ye waters that ' are a'bove the ' heavens.

5 Let them praise the ' Name of the ' Lord : for he spake the word and they were made, he commanded ' and they ' were cre'ated.

6 He hath made them fast for ' ever and ' ever : he hath given them a law ' which shall ' not be ' broken.

7 Praise the ' Lord upon ' earth : ye ' dragons and ' all ' deeps;

8 Fire and hail ' snow and ' vapours : wind and ' storm ful'filling his ' word;

9 Mountains and ' all ' hills : fruitful ' trees and ' all ' cedars;

10 Beasts and ' all ' cattle : worms and ' feath'ered ' fowls;

11 Kings of the earth and ' all ' people : princes and all ' judges ' of the ' world;

12 Young men and maidens, old men and children, praise the ' Name of the ' Lord : for his Name only is excellent, and his ' praise above ' heaven and ' earth.

2nd Part   13 He shall exalt the horn of his people, all his ' saints shall ' praise him : even the children of Israel, even the ' people that ' serveth ' him.

PSALM 149

W. CROTCH

241

O SING unto the Lord a ' new ' song : let the congre'gation of ' saints '
praise him.

2 Let Israel rejoice in ' him that ' made him : and let the children of
Sion be ' joyful ' in their ' King.

3 Let them praise his ' Name in the ' dance : let them sing praises
unto ' him with ' tabret and ' harp.

4 For the Lord hath pleasure ' in his ' people : and ' helpeth the '
meek-'hearted.

5 Let the saints be ' joyful with ' glory : let them re'joice ' in their '
beds.

6 Let the praises of God be ' in their ' mouth : and a ' two-edged '
sword in their ' hands;

7 To be avenged ' of the ' heathen : and ' to re'buke the ' people;

8 To bind their ' kings in ' chains : and their ' nobles with ' links of '
iron.

2nd 9 That they may be avenged of them, ' as it is ' written : Such '
Part honour have ' all his ' saints.

PSALM 150

242

O PRAISE God ' in his ' holiness : praise him in the ' firmament ' of his ' power.

2 Praise him in his ' noble ' acts : praise him ac'cording to his ' excellent ' greatness.

3 Praise him in the ' sound of the ' trumpet : praise him up'on the ' lute and ' harp.

4 Praise him in the ' cymbals and ' dances : praise him up'on the ' strings and ' pipe.

5 Praise him upon the ' well-tuned ' cymbals : praise him up'on the ' loud ' cymbals.

Unison 6 Let everything ' that hath ' breath : praise ' — ' — the ' Lord.